Reviving the
Heart

The Reverend Dr Richard Turnbull is Principal of
Wycliffe Hall, Oxford, and a member of the Faculty of
Theology of the University of Oxford.

Other publications
A Passionate Faith, Oxford: Monarch, 2012
Shaftesbury: The Great Reformer, Oxford: Lion, 2010
Anglican and Evangelical? London: Continuum, 2007
(reprinted 2010)

RICHARD TURNBULL

Reviving the Heart

THE
STORY OF THE
18TH CENTURY
REVIVAL

LION

A Lion Book
an imprint of
Lion Hudson plc
Wilkinson House, Jordan Hill Road,
Oxford OX2 8DR, England
www.lionhudson.com
ISBN 978 0 7459 5349 6 (print)
ISBN 978 0 7459 5892 7 (epub)
ISBN 978 0 7459 5891 0 (Kindle)
ISBN 978 0 7459 5893 4 (pdf)

First edition 2012
10 9 8 7 6 5 4 3 2 1 0

Typeset in 12/14 Perpetua
Printed in Great Britain by Clays Ltd, St Ives plc

Dedication

This book is dedicated to my wife, Caroline, and my children, Sarah, Katie, Matt, and Rebecca, with whom my love of history has been shared whether or not it was wanted. The stories of John and Charles Wesley, George Whitefield, and other pioneers have travelled with us on car journeys and accompanied our family meals. I am very grateful also to my commissioning editors, first Kate Kirkpatrick and then Ali Hull, to Jessica Tinker and Helen Birkbeck for their editorial work, and to Lion Hudson for publishing. I am also very grateful to Katie Hofman, my personal assistant, who prepared the terms for the index. The research was partially funded by a grant from the Latimer Trust and my thanks go to the Trustees for this support. The privilege of study leave from my post as Principal of Wycliffe Hall, Oxford, assisted immensely with the writing. I hope the students will benefit in due course.

Richard Turnbull
Oxford, Summer 2012

Contents

Foreword

"Why is it", asks Os Guinness, "that no movement of spiritual renewal has ever lasted longer than the third generation? Is it not partly because men forget so soon?" (*Doubt*, Lion Publishing, p. 62).

Perhaps it is this awareness that has prompted Richard Turnbull to give us desperately needed *reminders*, as he takes his readers on a captivating journey across some sixty of the most exciting and nation-changing years in Britain's history. As far as many modern observers and historical commentators are concerned, the eighteenth-century Revival – together with the Reformation two centuries earlier – might never have taken place at all. It is *history* that provides the educative building blocks for both society and church. It is *memory* that brings the vital lessons of the past into the present.

It is in the preservation of names – and the stories surrounding them – that *Reviving the Heart* so clearly demonstrates divine sovereignty at its most generous. How is it that widespread blessings can be granted from heaven out of the conversions to Christ of such separately placed and uninfluential persons as Grimshaw of Haworth, Fletcher of Madeley, and Walker of Truro? Yet, if a little reflection is given to one of the most dysfunctional families in all Scripture – that of Jacob – we can only recognize that this is the style of God... once we are faced by the visions of Revelation, which reveal the twelve children of Israel standing around the glory of the divine throne.

How was it that, from a collection of nonentities and workers in the Israeli fishing industry, there could have emerged a movement that was to *turn the world upside-down*?

The same pattern is apparent in the book before us. That a major spiritual awakening can be occasioned despite the limitations of its leaders – the mistakes, the rashly maintained romances, the disputes and divisions, the little conceits and painful rivalries – the message is plain enough:

> Brothers, think of what you were when you were
> called. Not many of you were wise by human
> standards; not many were influential; not many
> were of noble birth. But God chose the foolish
> things of the world to shame the wise…
> (1 Corinthians 1:26–27)

True, there were a few highly placed individuals who fanned the flames of the Revival, notably the redoubtable Countess of Huntingdon and, later, the playwright celebrity of London, Hannah More. The numerous cameos before us will certainly include the touching of the great and the good – and the consequent upturn in national standards and policies – but the chief emphasis is that here was a movement and message that was not so much *for* the common people as *of* the people. The effect of the message on the Kingswood miners is a case in point.

Many thousands of Londoners would turn up for Wesley and Whitefield on London's Blackheath – not far from the nearby public tennis courts – at a small hillock that has been preserved until today in its original state and is known as "Whitefield's Mount".

Gwennap Pit – the famous hollow in the earth resulting from a collapsed tin mine near Redruth in Cornwall – is still visited today as pilgrims relive the days when John Wesley would preach to the thousands who gathered to hear him. The Black Bull public house in Yorkshire's Haworth still stands – with its reminder of Grimshaw, the fiery "apostle of the north", sending his parishioners flying into church with the lash of his whip.

The numbers attending open-air preaching in the fields and highways were massive – and that in an overall population of no more than 9 million.

The preachers – whether it was in Bristol, Oxford, or London itself, or in Savannah far away in Georgia (for the pages before us helpfully set out the effects of the Awakening on both sides of the Atlantic) – were kept at full stretch. Often they would be required to preach five or six times a day. And the preaching could be feared. Samuel Walker of Truro was so powerful that parishioners would edge away from church – "Let us go, here comes Walker!"

How would we react to the banning of preachers in our own day? How might a fresh sovereign act of God in revival affect town and country alike? How may we prepare the ground for such a sovereign act to take place once again? We can surely believe, as we read the pages before us, that – although God never exactly repeats his wonders – *there will be a next time*!

RICHARD BEWES OBE
West London

CHAPTER 1

The origins of the
Evangelical Revival

The outbreak of what is now known as the Evangelical Revival was as surprising to the participants as it was to observers. It had a profound and lasting effect on English culture and society, as well as on the Church. Before we can tell the story we need to set the scene. Why did these events take place? What caused them?

What was the Revival and when did it happen?

Labels and dates are convenient for the historian, but can act like a sticky note covering up a more complicated picture. The Evangelical Revival (or "Awakening", the term used for the phenomenon in North America) is the name given to the series of events of intense religious fervour – local, regional, national, and international – in the middle decades of the eighteenth century. The Revival had a number of key distinguishing marks. The first was a recovery of a profound piety in personal devotion. The early participants rose early and prayed deeply and often. The second was a rejection of superficiality in faith in favour of more substantial beliefs and a new depth of self-examination. The focus was on the all-pervading impact of sin, and then, most importantly (and arguably a new feature of religious faith at the time), on thankfulness in response to what God had done. So John Wesley kept a diary indicating his daily "grace rating" – how he was doing! Third, there was a recovery of the doctrines of the Reformation, the essential beliefs of Protestantism. Two further distinguishing marks of the Revival, occurring perhaps not for the first time but certainly in a newly distinctive way, were a resurgence of expectation of the experience of God in the believer's life, and a passion to bring the message of the faith to all. So we have an intensity of devotion and faith plus classic doctrines combined with an experiential encounter with the divine, expressed in a transformation of life and a renewed passion for evangelism.

The preaching of the "new birth" – that is, of conversion – was probably the defining feature of the Revival, though there were antecedents.[1] Conversion did not happen for the first time in this period, but it did move centre stage. The Revival was characterized by relatively large numbers of people having a common experience of God's action in their heart in comparatively confined areas over a fairly short period of time. Mark Noll refers to "intense periods of unusual response to gospel preaching linked with unusual efforts at godly living".[2] Thomas Kidd invests the meaning with a more spiritual explanation by referring to "seasons of revival, or outpourings of the Holy Spirit".[3] Revival was bound by neither geography nor social class. Important aspects of the phenomenon can be discovered by considering both the local and the national and transnational perspectives. There were local revivals in various parts of Great Britain and the colonies, and regional outbreaks (or "outpourings", if the more spiritual interpretation is preferred) in Wales and parts of New England, which had a national impact on both sides of the Atlantic. John Wesley, comparing North America and England, remarked that the work in one place seemed to be identical to that in the other.[4]

The conversion of John Wesley (1703–91) in 1738 is often seen as a convenient date with which to mark the beginning of the Revival. However, it is both inadequate and inaccurate. Key individuals had already undergone this distinguishing characteristic of evangelical faith, including George Whitefield (1714–70), Howell Harris (1714–73), and Daniel Rowland (1713–90). In North America, Jonathan Edwards (1703–58) had already overseen an outbreak of revival in the town of Northampton, Massachusetts, in 1734, which later spread to other communities in the area of the Connecticut River valley.

The action of God did not distinguish between the social backgrounds of the recipients. The Revival was notable for a new intensity of religious conviction among both the poorest and the best-off in society. Indeed, conversions among the miners of the Kingswood district of Bristol and other deprived groups may have encouraged resistance from some elements of higher society and the Church. The privileged preferred order; conversion empowered the poor. Some of the more radical elements of the "Methodists" pushed the boundaries beyond what the leadership would tolerate. Within a century of the outbreaks the once-radical Methodists had become institutionalized and were expelling new radicals from their ranks – hence the emergence of the Primitive Methodists. Wesley always remained a Tory, a political conservative.

Some important and influential figures did, however, experience conversion, including two prominent women, Selina, Countess of Huntingdon (1707–91) and Hannah More (1745–1833). In this way the gospel reached at least some policy-makers and opinion-formers. Selina certainly met some resistance from her aristocratic friends, horrified by "enthusiasm" and disturbed by some of the more chaotic expressions of revival, but also fearful of disruption of the social order. The Duchess of Buckingham, writing to the Countess of Huntingdon, rather gave the game away: "Their doctrines are most repulsive and strongly tinctured with impertinence and disrespect towards their superiors, in perpetually endeavouring to level all ranks and do away with all distinctions."[5] However, not everything can be explained in terms of social history. The noble lady also made clear the challenge of the Revival doctrines: "It is monstrous to be told that you have a heart as sinful as the common wretches that crawl the earth."[6] The recovery of the Reformation doctrines (especially the idea of justification by faith alone – being put right with God on account of faith in Christ and his work) was a significant Revival feature. Equally socially disruptive to some were the phenomena that accompanied many of the events: an unruly cacophony of cries, swooning, and trances. Such things gave rise to varied interpretations, though generally there was a degree of healthy scepticism.

The Revival in England took place both within and without the Established Church. The Church of England was built on foundational documents: the Thirty-nine Articles of Religion set out certain basic doctrinal standards; the Book of Common Prayer contained the services of worship authorized by the Church; and the Ordinal was the service of ordination – hence revealing the Church's understanding of ministry. These doctrinal and liturgical writings (together with Archbishop Thomas Cranmer's *Book of Homilies*, that is, sermons) placed the Church of England firmly within the Calvinist traditions of the Protestant Reformation (in other words, its doctrine largely reflected the emphases of John Calvin of Geneva). However, the passing of time and the ebbs and flows of the history of the Church of England had left these key building blocks shrouded in at best a degree of mystery. For some clergy the Revival brought these roots back to prominence, and was thus instrumental in establishing the moderate Calvinist tradition on which Anglican evangelicalism was built. For others this was not so, as is shown by the development of Methodism as a separate denomination towards the end of the eighteenth century. In England there was also a considerable body of traditional religious dissenters (those who did not give their consent to the Established Church; sometimes called non-conformists). They too were affected by the Revival, Isaac Watts (1674–1748) the hymn writer being a notable example. However, much of the main action took place within the Church of England. In North America the dominant Presbyterianism was no less affected – indeed more so than the Established Church. Those influenced by the Awakenings were known as the "New Lights" – and those who resisted, the "Old Lights".

The Revival, in both Great Britain and North America, also employed new means of evangelism. Two prominent features were preaching and itinerancy. The proclamation of "new birth" or spiritual regeneration, required because of human sin and depravity, was central to the Revival's methodology. Sermons had become long, dry, moralistic rambles, but were now transformed by spiritual vitality and preaching to the heart as much as to the intellect. Also, in contrast to the usual model of preaching in a church, the practice of itinerancy developed — that is, the preacher or evangelist travelled from place to place to speak to large crowds, often in the open air. The picture was in reality more complicated. Some of the pioneers adopted the principles of itinerancy while others remained faithful to parish boundaries. Itinerancy was controversial within the Established Church, where it was viewed with suspicion and disdain. Without the permission of the incumbent, it was illegal to preach in his parish. For most of the early Revival preachers, while the pulpits were closed, the fields were open.

The Revival can thus be characterized as the religion of the heart, a Protestant awakening, or even a work of God. It had a wide range of social, political, ecclesiastical, and psychological aspects. The weight given to any one or combination of these factors rather depends on the approach adopted by the historian. If the Revival is simply portrayed as the work of God, then why within two years of Wesley's conversion did the group of Christians with which he was most closely associated (the Moravians) split in two, and why did Wesley and Whitefield fall out so ferociously? This is perhaps a rather unusual way for the Lord of history to operate. The Revival can also be fully understood only by appreciating its place within a global context, recognized much more now than previously. Both Wesley and Whitefield, two of the central players in the story, were as well known in the North American colonies as in England. Each of them made regular visits, caused controversy for a variety of reasons, and found the pulpits of the Established Church closed to them, despite being ordained ministers of the Church of England. European as well as North American influences are also central to understanding what took place.

The state of religion in England

The classic understanding, propagated mostly by those within the evangelical movement, is that the Revival was essentially a reaction to the condition of society and faith in the early eighteenth century. Indeed, the state of faith had declined rapidly (at least as seen through the rose-tinted spectacles of the later evangelical commentators) from the high point of the Commonwealth period; that is, during the Puritan ascendancy represented by the Cromwellian Protectorate of 1653–59. This was the case despite the nation being saved from Catholicism by William of Orange's accession to the throne in 1688. The day was dark, the embers of faith were low; it was time for God to act. The case is put explicitly, if uncritically, in one of the earlier "house histories" of evangelicalism: "the drunkenness of the age is proverbial", the "country squires were sodden with alcohol", "filth was regarded as the choicest form of wit", and, as for the Church, "only the cautious and colourless remained, Laodicians, whose ideal Church was neither hot nor cold".[7] The Church "had forgotten its mission, unspiritual, discredited, useless".[8]

How accurate is this picture? There has been a reaction against the claim that the Church in the pre-Revival period lacked faith and sophistication. The nation and the Church both emerged from the conflagration of 1649–62 (the Civil Wars, execution of Charles I, the Commonwealth, and the Restoration) in need of breathing space. A king had been executed and then his house restored, Puritan faith established and then repudiated. The matter was settled with the Glorious Revolution of 1688. The nation was to remain Protestant, but perhaps in a slightly more polite way.

The classic explanations

The standard approach was set out by John Walsh in an essay published in 1966, in which he identified three main categories into which explanations of the Revival fall.

The first of these was the continuing influence of high-church spiritual piety. This requires some explanation. The high-church spiritual tradition of the early eighteenth century was considerably different from what was subsequently termed "high church" in the light of the Anglo-Catholic renewal movement of the nineteenth century. High-church orthodoxy in the period after 1688 had a number of characteristics. The tradition was not Roman Catholic and not especially sympathetic to Catholicism. The loyalty of its adherents was not in doubt. Considerable weight was given to the Church and its continuing tradition. So there was a tendency to look to significant bishops (e.g. Lancelot Andrewes) and the divines of the Stuart period, Jeremy Taylor and George Herbert, if not to the monarchs. Some doubted the legitimacy of William of Orange and hence declined to swear the necessary oaths (as the Puritans had done before them in 1660), and so acquired the name "non-jurors". In short, the high-church group remained Protestant and orthodox, but eclectic and wedded to the royal supremacy (even though there was some disagreement over which monarchy). Walsh describes their adherence to "apostolic order, continuity, authority and discipline of the visible Church, the necessity of apostolic succession",[9] together with baptism, Eucharist, and liturgical conformity. It is no surprise that some of these efforts and desires for spiritual vitality formed part of the background to the Revival. The usual example given is that of William Law (1686–1761). His early works, especially *A Serious Call to a Devout and Holy Life* (1729), represented the classic high-church description of holiness, requiring dedication and discipline of life. This book certainly influenced both of the Wesleys and the other members of the Holy Club in Oxford (see Chapter 2). That is hardly surprising. It was not an evangelical work. As we will see, the Awakening was something of a reaction to it, rather than a continuation.

The second group of explanations saw the outbreak as a reaction against Protestant rationalism and a protest against arid intellectualism and the perceived cold formality of much of contemporary religiosity. This was reflected in sermons – long (indeed, *very* long), dry articulations of obscure points of theology. There seemed to be very little for the soul. In many ways this was a reflection of the age, with the advance of Enlightenment thinking, and the elevation of the mind and carefully constructed argument. Wesley commented that faith "is not barely a speculative, rational thing, a cold lifeless assent, a train of ideas in the head, but also a disposition of the heart".[10] The reaction to rationality was exemplified in the appeal to experience. Presbyterianism in North America – old-fashioned dissent – was increasingly influenced by rationality. Some even abandoned Trinitarian faith altogether. Wesley and Whitefield were seen as reacting against this trend.[11]

The third type of explanation emphasized direct continuity with the Puritan tradition, reviving pre-existing Christian doctrines, and taking its adherents down well-known and recognizable paths with familiar guides. The continuities are many. Despite the ebbs and flows it is now accepted by many scholars, in particular Patrick Collinson, that throughout the history of the Church of England a continuing Puritan tradition remained within it. So the Revival can be represented as Puritanism coming back to life. Certainly many of the spiritual and doctrinal works that featured in the Revival, and indeed in the personal stories of many of the participants, came from the Puritan stable and the Puritan divines. The classic appeal to the formularies of the Church of England also reflected this approach. The theology of the Revival clearly mirrored that of the Reformation, more so with Whitefield and the progress of the Revival within the Established Church than with Wesley and the development of Methodism.

However, there are also difficulties. Whitefield cut through some of the rationalistic, systematic theology of the Puritans to preach and proclaim the "new birth". This was a new appeal that placed much more emphasis on individual experience of the power of the Spirit in the heart than previously. Indeed, in some ways Whitefield was much more radical, concerned for field preaching and even church planting (though the phrase is an anachronism), and less so for church order and doctrinal confessions.

The problem with Walsh's original essay is that it leaves the impression that the Revival came about as a result of some sort of combination of these factors, a synthesis. This approach is inadequate, but, before looking at a new framework, there remains one crucial aspect to consider.

International connections

The Revival was not simply an isolated phenomenon restricted to Great Britain. There were many influences from other parts of the world, especially continental Europe and North America. Much greater recognition is now given to these international aspects. There was communication between friends and contacts, together with the exchange of news about people and events. As immigration increased from Europe, so too did the links. With England's heritage as a Protestant country, it is not surprising that the movements of peoples across Europe, caused by what was seen as Catholic oppression, led to greater sympathy for the victims and perhaps even greater openness to the influence of Revival. The expulsion of Protestants from Salzburg in 1731 was a particular case in point.

The role of Pietism in central Europe is particularly important. From this movement emerged the Moravian Church, especially in the form fostered by the significant but eccentric Count Nicholas von Zinzendorf (1700–66). He was born into a Pietist family and educated at Halle. In 1722 he offered refuge to a number of persecuted Protestants from Moravia and Bohemia and allowed them to build the village of *Herrnhut* ("the Lord's Watch") on his estate at Berthelsdorf. During the 1720s the village began to attract groups of like-minded people, and the classic features of such communities began to emerge: a press, schools, and a community house. The worship and daily life sought to reflect those of Acts 2: communal living and informality in prayer and worship. Other developments included, in 1735, a new Moravian settlement in the North American colony of Georgia. This settlement, together with stories of oppression at the hands of the Catholic authorities of central Europe, brought the Pietists a new prominence and attracted the attention of figures such as Gilbert Tennent and Jonathan Edwards, prominent Presbyterian pastors in North America. In this way continental Pietism was connected to key figures of the Revival in England and the American colonies. Pietism was essentially a renewal movement. It embraced elements of theology that were central to the Revival, but also some mystical emphases and practices from Catholicism which were far removed from traditional Calvinism. There were also complex divisions between the main protagonists. The promotion of inner godliness, hymnody, personal encounter, and new birth had a significant influence on the Revival, yet certain elements of Pietism ("the wounds of Jesus", "quietness or stillness") did not sit well with an England where Calvinism and Puritanism remained formative for the national Church.

Across the Atlantic there were stirrings before Revival broke out in England. There was a long-standing Puritan heritage in North America. We have already noted how this led to division between the traditionalists and those who embraced revival. However, despite the differences, international Calvinism also provided a channel of communication. So when Jonathan Edwards sought to tell the story of Revival in Northampton in 1733–35 – *A Faithful Narrative of the Surprising Work of God* – it was two England-based Calvinist dissenters, Isaac Watts and John Guyse, who published the work in London. This helped ensure that Revival and Calvinism remained partners. The settlement of Moravians in Georgia and the visit by John and Charles Wesley also helped bring the relevant forces and individuals in contact with each other.

By placing the Revival in England in a wider context, we can see how differing influences came to bear on its various aspects. The international links between North America, Great Britain, and continental Europe provided a ready flow of information but also raised consciousness, brought participants into contact with one another, and prepared the ground for the work of God in all its diversity.

A new framework

The story of the Revival, its personalities and key events, and its impact on people, both individuals and communities, is an exciting one. However, it cannot be understood without both context and interpretation. The traditional explanations have changed in the light of more recent scholarship. Inevitably there remains a degree of tension between "providential" approaches that stress the Revival as an act of God and more "secular" understandings that seek alternative cultural, social, and political causes. The two approaches should not be presented as an either/or choice. We can easily dismiss the extremes – either an outpouring of the Spirit of God without reference to other aspects, or the failure to recognize that the wide range of factors that led to Revival cannot explain everything. The explanation of "a surprising work of God" may be seen as providential by some and psychological by others; there still remains the essential task of setting out and elucidating the events, their impact, and their meaning.

One of the complexities in seeking to understand and explain the origins of the Protestant awakenings of the early eighteenth century is the tendency to present the reader with a vast array of differing options. Historians today are less likely to opt for a single explanatory narrative (no doubt rightly so), but neither does that mean that explanations of events can simply be seen as some sort of convergence of various alternatives.

We have explored the classic explanation that the origins of the Revival lay in high churchmanship, a reaction to rationalism, and a reawakening of the Puritan tradition. Each of these has merit, but also poses difficulty. The link of the Evangelical Revival to high churchmanship continues to be asserted but is something of a confusion of category. Walsh correctly notes that high churchmen being converted were deserting their principles. Similarly, we have seen that the relationship to rationalism was not simply a reaction. The more recent scholarship has re-emphasized the importance of the international dimension, with regard to both communication links and, of course, the influence of continental Pietism.

Perhaps we can reassess the traditional approach? There were three distinct themes in the background to the Revival. The first of these was *reaction to moralism*. Orthodox, moralistic sermons were key elements of both the high churchmanship and the rationalism that pervaded the period before the Awakenings. The important point is not the high-church tradition or rationalism per se, but that both offered solutions that were essentially moralistic. The exhortation was to live a better life, to be more devoted to spiritual exercises, or to become more pious. This is what evangelicals reacted against because it both proved inadequate and sat awkwardly with the Reformation doctrines. The second key source then was *reclaiming doctrine*. The Revival cannot be seen simply as the reassertion of Puritanism and yet that tradition, including its Calvinism, featured strongly. Indeed, the combination of an inadequate moralism and the reclaiming of the Reformed doctrine of justification by faith alone go hand in hand. The third crucial element is that of *appropriating experience*. Specifically this came about through the influence of continental Pietism and played itself out in the Revival themes of "new birth" and "conversion". The experiential encounter was a personal one, a truly transformational meeting with God. The origins of the Revival lie in the combination and meeting of these three great themes: reacting against mere moralism, reclaiming Reformation doctrine, and appropriating experience.

The transcontinental connections, between England, North America, and Europe, provided channels of communication through which stories were transmitted. The movement of people and population contributed to the meetings of individuals, the recognition of shared experiences, and different emphases in the various parts of the Revival. So different individuals were more or less affected by the Calvinist international – that is, the friendships and intercontinental communication channels between Calvinists (for example, the story of the Northampton Revival coming to England via dissenting Calvinist ministers) – or by Moravian Pietism (for example, John and Charles Wesley's encounter with the Moravian Christians).

The uniqueness of the Revival stems from each of these elements; the distinctiveness of the various aspects derives from their relative weight. We now turn to the story, to the narrative of the Revival itself, with all its twists and turns, its excitements, personalities, and complexities.

CHAPTER 2

The rectory and the inn

Two names dominate the story of the Revival. Their interwoven friendship and conflict, together with their place in the development of different strands of the Revival, have governed the writing of the histories. Other players must be allowed to flourish too, but we have to begin with John Wesley and George Whitefield. Their backgrounds and upbringing in one sense could not seem more different: the former a son of the rectory, the latter born in an inn. However, the differences in social background should not be exaggerated. Wesley and Whitefield have both been subjected to "providential history" – that is, writing history from God's point of view. So the young John Wesley was snatched from a burning fire in an act of God, a special deliverance, which became, as Ralph Waller put it, one of the building blocks of Methodism.[1] Indeed, in the epitaph he composed in 1753 when he thought he was dying, Wesley described himself as "a Brand plucked out of the burning".[2] Whitefield's *Journals* include "A Short Account of God's Dealings with the Reverend Mr George Whitefield". They are an invaluable source, but were written after the event and cover only the period up to 1745. Indeed, later editions show signs of the editorial pen.

Some have argued that Whitefield's lack of insight into his own private life and writings, when compared with Wesley's *Journals* and extensive works and his legacy in Methodism, means that Wesley has eclipsed Whitefield. That view has some weight. Wesley is increasingly recognized as a complex character, so radical and yet so conservative. The same John Wesley who when he ordained workers for the American colonies declared, "I conceive myself at full liberty, as I violate no order and invade no man's right by appointing and sending labourers into the harvest,"[3] also said, "I live and die a member of the Church of England."[4] Whitefield's organizational skills may have been less honed than those of Wesley, but his eloquence and powerful use of gesture in preaching (hence Harry Stout's referring to him as "The Divine Dramatist"[5]), his fascinating relationship with Selina, Countess of Huntingdon, and his theological disputation with Wesley had a deep and lasting influence on the Church of England. We must also remember there were two famous Wesleys, Charles as well as John, along with pioneers in the parishes and conversions among the landed gentry as well as the miners of Kingswood. The real history of the Revival will allow all these voices to be heard.

The birth and upbringing of John Wesley

John Wesley was born at Epworth Rectory in Lincolnshire on 17 June 1703. He was born to Samuel and Susanna Wesley. In many ways the rectory household reflected the pious yet somewhat dry high-church orthodoxy that John Wesley both embraced and reacted against. His father and mother were both born into dissenting families that had suffered at the Great Ejection of 1662, when some 2,000 clergy were expelled from their livings with the Restoration of Charles II. The Wesleys had become rather high-church members of the Established Church by conviction. There was some marital conflict over the authenticity of William of Orange's claim to the throne: Susanna viewed William as a usurper and thought that the rightful line was that of James II; Samuel swore an oath of loyalty to William. Adam Clarke recorded in 1836 John Wesley's description of his parents falling out over prayer: "Why did you not say *amen* this morning to the prayer for the King?" Samuel reportedly said to Susanna, to get the reply, "I do not believe the Prince of Orange to be King." Samuel's extraordinary response was, "If we have two Kings, we must have two beds."[6] Although the succession of Anne in 1702 seems to have restored marital harmony, the argument between them was not resolved. Nevertheless, one outcome was the birth of John. So his parents were high Tories as well as high church, despite the differing weight given to claimants for the throne.

Samuel did not lack piety and was concerned about the drift in the Established Church towards deism (that is, a belief in a supreme being, a God, but nothing more). As Rector of Epworth, with a population of some 1,100 people, he saw it as his duty to teach the faith to his parishioners. He was also concerned for their social well-being, and founded voluntary societies to provide social care. Yet it was tough going: the village was isolated and there was opposition to his ministry. Samuel's downfall was debt. He was a bad manager of money and owed a considerable sum by the time of John's birth. His predicament was compounded by not receiving the full value of the living (in other words, the tithes and rents due to him), and by having a large family (John was the fifteenth child of nineteen, though only seven survived). He also backed the wrong side in an election in 1705, which led to the demand for the immediate repayment of a loan by a benefactor. Unable to repay the loan, Samuel was imprisoned, albeit briefly, in Lincoln Castle. In prison he led prayers and preached and worked with the Society for Promoting Christian Knowledge to arrange the distribution of books. It was a wretched time which he bore with some grace, but the cloud of debt was ever present over the rectory.

Susanna was a godly woman. She even convened a group in the parish to discuss sermons. In this forerunner of a Methodist class meeting, Susanna in time gathered around her some 200 parishioners: "Our company increased every night; for I dare deny none that ask admittance. Last Sunday, I believe, we had above two hundred. And yet many went away, for want of room to stand."[7] Samuel was concerned about such activities, and when the parish curate accused Susanna of holding a "conventicle" – an illegal gathering in a home for worship under the terms of the Clarendon Code, a series of Acts of Parliament passed to suppress dissent in the aftermath of the ejections of 1662 – she was not amused. Such activity, she claimed, did not reflect badly upon Samuel, "because your wife endeavours to draw people to church. For my part I value no censure upon this account," and because her concern was to "advance the glory of God or the salvation of souls".[8]

So the family into which John was born, and also, of course, his brother Charles in 1707, was fairly typical of a clerical household of the time. There was prayer and piety, an orthodoxy of faith, and an overarching Tory view of the world which expressed itself in loyalty to the monarchy (even if *which* monarch was occasionally in dispute), and a concern for the poor. Although the household was not wealthy, Samuel and Susanna sought to bring their children up in the knowledge of God and to faithfully serve the call to ministry in the Church.

The fire at Epworth Rectory in 1709 completely destroyed the building, and it was a miracle that no one died. The sense of divine providence, the intervention of God to save the family, was certainly true at the time, but its particular application to the rescue of John developed with hindsight. The fire broke out in the late evening, between 11 p.m. and midnight, and spread rapidly. Susanna ascribed it to an unknown accident; others, rather less probably, to disgruntled parishioners. She escaped through the front of the house while Samuel evacuated the children into the back garden and several times tried to reach John, who was trapped upstairs and who was rescued from the outside. Naturally, Wesley's later biographers had a field day. As we noted, Wesley himself adopted the phrase "a Brand plucked out of the burning", which, along with the entire rise of Methodism, became part of the providential history. It was the motto for his *Journals* and adorned paintings of the rectory fire.

In 1732 John asked Susanna to set down the methods she had used, and was later admired for, in educating and bringing up her family. Her reply showed her concern for discipline and order: the use of the rod ensured the children would be taught "to cry softly", so that the "most odious noise of the crying of children was rarely heard in the house".[9] The poverty of the household clearly did not extend to an inability to employ a maid, for it was to her that the children were to whisper (not call) if they needed anything. Perhaps more in line with modern parenting (or maybe not...), the children had to eat what was set before them, were not allowed to snack between meals, and were left awake in their rooms until they fell asleep (in bed by eight). The aim was "to conquer their will, and bring them to an obedient temper".[10] As soon as they could speak they were taught the Lord's Prayer, which was recited twice a day. Susanna added that "never were children in better order... till that fatal dispersion of them, after the fire, into several families".[11] After the fire the rectory was rebuilt in less than a year, but in Susanna's eyes damage had been done to the family bond.

John entered Charterhouse at the age of ten. Looking back in his *Journal* at the time of his conversion (with all the attendant problems that brings), he claimed that he was more negligent of his religious duties at this time, though still attending morning and evening prayer and reading the Scriptures. He described himself as hoping for salvation by not being as bad as others, and diligent in the duties of religion. This account was undoubtedly influenced by his later conversion experience. John went up to study at Christ Church, Oxford, in 1720 – when our next figure, George Whitefield, was just six.

The birth and upbringing of George Whitefield

George Whitefield had a very different upbringing and early years from John Wesley. The Bell Inn was in the centre of Gloucester, and it is here that he was born on 16 December 1714 to Thomas and Elizabeth. He was the youngest of seven children. The business had prospered. George himself looked back on his infancy in his *Journal*, written in 1739. As with Wesley, Whitefield's view is shaped by the supreme advantage of hindsight invested with divine providence. Especially excruciating was the claim to be following "the example of my dear Saviour, who was born in a manger belonging to an inn".[12] However, the *Journal* is a crucial source and does reveal details of his early childhood and character. He noted that his mother had endured fourteen weeks of sickness after his birth and that his father died when he was two. These are important facts. The prosperity of the Bell and indeed of the family declined rapidly after Thomas's death. Whitefield made much of the sins of his youth, referring to stealing from his mother, playing cards, and engaging in "roguish tricks". He added that he had an early fondness for being a clergyman and that he "used frequently to imitate the ministers reading prayers".[13] He stated that he gave some of the money he stole to the poor; we have no way of assessing the veracity of this claim. He was thankful for his mother's care for his education and that she protected him from being drawn into the public side of the family business – presumably meaning the Bell. He also thanked his schoolmaster "for the great pains he took with me and his other scholars, in teaching us to speak and write correctly".[14] He made good progress in the classics.

The family's circumstances were, however, declining. In 1722, some six years after his father's death and when George was eight, his mother Elizabeth married for a second time. Her new husband was ironmonger Capel Longden. George understated the problem in his *Journal* when he said that "it proved what the world would call an unhappy match",[15] though he also claimed that God overruled for good. The disaster affected both personal life and the business domain. Longden was reasonably wealthy and a member of the same church as the Whitefields, St Mary de Crypt. He and Elizabeth tussled immediately over control of the business at the Bell, and the fortunes of both family and business diminished significantly. One consequence was that a university education for George was now out of the question. He began to work at the Bell. For a year and a half he "put on my blue apron... washed mops, cleaned rooms".[16] He described the break-up of the marriage simply by saying that his "mother was obliged to leave the inn".[17] The business was then put into the hands of George's brother Richard, who sought to remove any trace of Longden from the Bell. Elizabeth took a cottage while George continued to work as an assistant at the inn. He fell out with his sister-in-law, however, though it is of course only with the advantage of providential hindsight that he was able to say that "God, by this means was forcing me out of the public business and calling me from drawing wine for drunkards, to draw water out of the wells of salvation for the refreshment of His spiritual Israel".[18]

George then spent two months in Bristol before returning to Gloucester to live with his mother. He described his lifestyle at this time as reading plays, sauntering from place to place, and adorning the body, but not the soul. Despite all this the possibility emerged of entering Oxford as a servitor, and George re-entered school. Being a servitor was the poor man's way into eighteenth-century Oxford. Tuition was free, but in return the servitor looked after three or four other students, undertaking duties that ranged from running errands to cleaning shoes. They were looked down on and stood out from the main student body by distinctive dress, status, and convention. They were not allowed to attend the same classes or to receive Holy Communion with the other students. But it opened the door.

George's inner conflicts continued. He returned to his schooling with some vigour but was soon dragged back into "the school of the Devil" by falling in with the wrong company. Again he saw God intervening to save him from a "full career to hell",[19] and returned to a pattern of religiosity. Just before his eighteenth birthday, he entered Oxford.

Both John Wesley and George Whitefield viewed their early years and upbringing through the eyes of their later experience of God, which undoubtedly coloured their interpretation of events. Their childhoods and youth displayed many similarities, yet much in their background was different. Hence the conflicts of religiosity and indulgence went on in both of them: one the son of a rectory, the other a child of the inn. The fact that neither had yet attained the religious assurance that was one of the hallmarks of the Evangelical Revival shows that their religious experience was that of their pre-conversion state, and, in that respect, their struggles were typical of the age.

Oxford and the Holy Club

By the time George Whitefield entered Pembroke College, in 1732, John Wesley was already a Fellow of Lincoln College. The college Fellowships consisted of unmarried tutors, usually ordained, who very often later succeeded to livings (parish appointments) under the control of the Fellowship. Wesley had entered Christ Church in 1720 as an undergraduate, indeed as an Exhibitioner. There is some, albeit rather scant, information about his years there, contained in exchanges of letters with his mother. He mentioned his tutors and showed a clear concern for the supernatural – with stories of transportation and apparition. Money remained a problem – he apparently kept his hair long to reduce costs – and he received financial support not only from his Exhibition but also from his brother Samuel.[20] The correspondence also dealt with the question of whether he should seek ordination. He was unsure, however, about his own motives. His mother wanted some help for his father. John was worried that he might seek ordination simply as a means to an income. His father summarized the complexity of pre-Revival English church life when he noted that, first, there was nothing wrong with that desire; second, it was better to live a more strict religious life; and, third, the glory and service of God should be the chief motive.[21] Wesley submitted to ordination. On the Friday before he was made a deacon he had breakfast with his tutor and then subscribed to the Articles. On the Saturday he read sermons and spent time in self-examination, and was ordained deacon on Sunday 19 September 1725. He was ordained as a presbyter (now often referred to as a priest) three years later. During this period he also spent a significant amount of time in coffee houses – some things in Oxford change little.[22]

In February 1726 he received his MA degree and in March he was elected to a vacant Fellowship at Lincoln College. Over the next two or three years he studied, sought to deepen his religious life, conducted prayers in the college chapel, and preached in his father's parishes, also providing general pastoral assistance. His diaries, begun in 1725, give some insight. Having hired a horse for transport he preached at Shipton, which included conducting both a baptism and a marriage, and also at Thame, Evesham, Stanton, Buckland, and Binsey. The record is perfunctory – setting out the conduct of duty rather than any religious impact. One feature of these early diaries is that they were peppered with religious injunctions; for example, he used Greek abbreviations to express thanks and praise and prayer. Wesley also enjoyed the social life of a Fellow. On the domestic front, his relationships with women were complicated throughout his life; in these early years in Oxford, Sally Kirkham, Betty Kirkham, Mary Pendarves, and Kitty Hargreaves all featured. Henry Rack notes that Wesley's sister "thought there was more than spirituality to all this".[23]

From 1727 to 1729 Wesley was engaged in parish work at Epworth, returning to Oxford at the end of November 1729 at the behest of the college Rector, as part of a campaign to improve both the academic and the moral standards of the university. Non-residence was common. During his absence his brother Charles had gone up to Oxford, also to Christ Church. On his return John, Charles, Robert Kirkham, and William Morgan began to meet regularly for religious discussions on Sunday evenings. We see in the early life of both Wesley and Whitefield this constant quest for religious righteousness, seriousness, and attention to the religious life. We observe a commendable earnestness – though, of course, as yet nothing approaching the doctrines of assurance and salvation that even now lay several years in the future. We have, however, found the Holy Club.

Immediately after his ordination Wesley resolved to review his life twice a day. In December 1729 he expressed concern about breaching his vows and failing to fix days of mortification – he resolved to fast every Wednesday.[24]

Concerned about whether he loved women more than God, in September 1726 he resolved again to fast monthly. His reading included Jeremy Taylor – not least his *Rules for Holy Living and Dying* – and *The Imitation of Christ* by Thomas à Kempis. The struggle continued day in, day out, month in, month out, year in, year out.

The spiritual and religious struggles of the four who constituted the Holy Club were thrown into sharp relief by the death of William Morgan in 1732. In less than three years the group and its activities had come to such prominence that there were quickly rumours, even allegations, that Morgan's death was the result of ascetic practices. In a letter to Richard Morgan, William's father, in October 1732, Wesley refuted the allegation that "my brother and I had killed your son"[25] as a result of the rigorous fasting he had adopted on their advice. In this letter John also gave something of the background to the Holy Club. He noted that when he returned to Oxford in 1729, "your son, my brother, myself, and one more agreed to spend three or four evenings in a week together. Our design was to read over the classics, which we had read in private, on common nights, and on Sunday some book in divinity."[26] The group also engaged in both prison and sick visiting – though only with the permission of the minister of any person receiving a visit, and indeed of the bishop himself. Kirkham reported to Wesley that the Holy Club had become a subject of amusement at his college (Merton), with both himself and their practices targeted.

Like so many labels, Holy Club was used mainly as a derogatory term, though Samuel Wesley at the end of 1730 referred to John as the father of the Holy Club and himself as the grandfather.[27] The group – now expanded to five – agreed to take the sacrament (that is, Holy Communion) as often as possible, once a week being the norm, and to continue their social work. Wesley also referred to other disparaging titles that were used: Sacramentarians, the Godly Club, the Enthusiasts, or the Reforming Club. Wesley himself simply used the description "our Company". To the sacramental and social practices of the club, a third was added – observing the fasts of the Church. This whole methodical approach led inevitably to the name "Methodists". Wesley had set out a methodical timetable in 1722 and his first proper diary, in 1725, contained numerous rules and resolutions. The Holy Club was nothing if not disciplined and systematic. The name "Methodist", used from the early days by critics, stuck and was later, after his conversion, accepted by Wesley himself.

George Whitefield was prime material for the Holy Club. Like Wesley, he constantly experienced the inner conflict and struggle of daily temptation and the desire to live a religious life. Before arriving at Oxford he was already reading William Law's *A Serious Call to a Devout and Holy Life*. Soon after his arrival he noted, "I now began to pray and sing psalms thrice every day."[28] The Methodists were despised but Whitefield wrote that he had "loved them before I came to the University; and so strenuously defended them when I heard them reviled by the students, that they began to think that I also in time should be one of them".[29] He reported struggling for a year with his desire to be truly acquainted with them, and when he saw them passing through a mocking crowd on the way to Communion he felt compelled to follow their example.

Whitefield sought the Wesleys' assistance in the case of a woman in the workhouse who had attempted suicide, while keeping his own name out of the proceedings. The woman concerned, however, disclosed it to Charles Wesley and he invited Whitefield to breakfast. Both Whitefield and Wesley looked back on the occasion as a divine appointment. Slowly Charles Wesley introduced Whitefield to the Holy Club; as Whitefield put it, by "degrees, he introduced me to the rest of his Christian brethren".[30] He noted how they built him up in both knowledge and holiness. Whitefield now joined in the fasts and regular receipt of Holy Communion, and engaged in works of charity. He commented in his *Journal*:

> Never did persons, I believe, strive more earnestly to enter in at the strait gate. They kept their bodies under, even to an extreme. They were dead to the world, and willing to be accounted as the dung and offscouring of all things, so that they might win Christ.[31]

Georgia

The colony of Georgia was established by Royal Charter in 1732. One of the trustees was John Burton of Corpus Christi College, Oxford. In the summer of 1735 John Wesley met some of the Georgia trustees after an approach by Burton, who was concerned to ensure proper spiritual provision for the colony. The previous year John had declined to take over the living of Epworth from his father, who died in the spring of 1735. On one level the decision to go to Georgia seems hasty, even impulsive. Part of the reason appears to have been "out of a pious design to convert the Indians".[32] Indeed, saving his own soul also mattered greatly to John. The Wesleys, however, even before their conversion, cannot be written off as simply working to gain their own salvation.

John had been elected to membership of the Society for Promoting Christian Knowledge; their passion was genuine and their horizon large. Why not Georgia?

Within a few months four men – the two Wesleys together with Benjamin Ingham and Charles Delamotte – set sail from Gravesend. The date was 14 October 1735. Charles had been ordained both deacon and presbyter a few weeks earlier. On board the ship there were twenty-six Moravians among the prospective colonists. John began at once to learn German so that he could converse with them. His *Journal* reveals that he busied himself with religious activities ranging from presiding over baptism and Communion to prayer, reading Scripture, and religious conversation. Both Wesleys declined to eat meat.

The voyage was eventful. It took over two weeks to reach the Isle of Wight! Finally, after several attempts, they left Cowes on 10 December – though it took them a full seven hours to pass the Needles. They weathered several storms in the following ten days: "Every ten minutes came a shock against the stern or side of the ship, which one would think should dash the planks in a thousand pieces."[33] Wesley's journal entry for this day also reveals how he viewed and began to relate to the Moravians ("the Germans", as he put it). He noted: "I had long before observed the great seriousness of their behaviour."[34] He observed their humility, their loving service of other passengers in ways "which none of the English would undertake",[35] and their calm faithfulness in God – especially when the storm broke the mainsail – compared to the screaming and trembling among the English. The eventful voyage continued with calmer and stormy weather alternating. On 4 March 1736 they sighted land. The next afternoon they sailed into the Savannah River. On Friday 6 March, almost five months after leaving England, "I first set my foot on American ground."[36] From this small island, they took a boat to Savannah. He stepped foot on English soil again just under two years later.

Wesley's time in Georgia was eventful. From August Spangenberg, who had led the first group of Bohemian Brethren to Georgia, he discovered more about Count von Zinzendorf, the Pietist tradition, and the establishment of Herrnhut. He compiled a collection of hymns and dealt with pastoral difficulties – not least the confession by two women to Charles, who returned to England in the summer of 1736, that they had had affairs with the governor, James Oglethorpe.

John was diligent, leading public prayer, preaching, and undertaking pastoral ministry among the congregation – "I began visiting my parishioners in order, from house to house…" – which he did for three hours a day.[37] He helped with poor relief and sought to engage the native Indians. Disastrously, he also became involved with an 18-year-old woman, Sophia Hopkey. He confessed to his brother Charles (who was ministering in Frederica, around eighty miles south of Savannah, as well as acting as secretary to Governor Oglethorpe) in a letter dated March 1736 – in Greek to disguise the content: "I stand in jeopardy every hour. Two or three women, younger, refined, God-fearing. Pray that I know none of them after the flesh."[38] The request was not entirely convincing. We know that in August "Miss Sophy" was in his afternoon society and he was reading to her from his diary. They had first met in March of that year, when Sophia was engaged to a rather disreputable man by the name of Mellichamp. She appears at various points in the *Journal*, almost casually at times. Wesley confessed to mixed intentions.[39] His conversation with her uncle, Thomas Causton, did not amount to a request for her hand, but that certainly seemed to be the direction of travel. There are references to John and Sophia praying and singing, and John acknowledging the danger when he escorted her by boat from Frederica to Savannah. It is quite difficult to untangle the web. Curnock (the editor of Wesley's *Journals*) claims that Sophia secretly loved Wesley. In November 1736, John said, "Miss Sophy, I should think myself happy if I was to spend my life with you."[40] Sophia promptly burst into tears and confessed her unhappiness with her own situation. On 1 November he wrote a long entry in his diary extolling her virtues. He wondered whether he should break off contact. He did not do so, and she came to his home every morning and evening for tutoring in French, reading sermons, prayer, and a psalm. Wesley admitted, "It was not long before I found it a task too hard for me to preserve the same intention with which I begun, in such intimacy of conversation as ours was."[41] At one point of separation he wrote, "My heart was with Miss Sophy all the time. I longed to see her, were it but for a moment."[42] On 27 February, after a conversation about a possible return to England, he took her by the hand and thought of engagement, and then resolved to avoid touch. On other occasions he seems to have put his arm around her waist and also kissed her.[43]

Sophia's intentions were also complex. Having jettisoned Mellichamp she then became the object of the desires of a Mr Williamson. It is not entirely clear how she felt about Wesley, though she seems to have been of the view that the clergy should remain single. Ralph Waller claims that, after rejecting Mellichamp, Sophia paused for Wesley to make his proposal – which he did not – and only after that did she announce her engagement to William Williamson. They were married on 12 March 1737. The relationship between Wesley and Williamson deteriorated rapidly, not least because Wesley was intent on maintaining his pastoral relationship with Sophia.

On 7 August 1737 a simple note in his *Journal* stated that he had refused to admit Sophia to Holy Communion. Wesley cited her infrequent attendance at Communion and neglect of public service and of fasting. More pertinently, he accused her of dissembling over her intentions regarding both Mellichamp and Williamson. This was unconvincing pastoral work on Wesley's part. The day after he refused Sophia Communion, she and Williamson issued a writ against Wesley for damages of £1,000 for defamation and refusal to admit to Communion without just cause. He denied the court's right to interrogate him over an ecclesiastical offence. The assembled Grand Jury was packed with his opponents, or, as he put it, with Dissenters, a Papist and an Infidel! The jury found ten charges for him to answer, though twelve of the forty-four jurors dissented. Hearings were constantly put off. Wesley decided to leave Georgia for England and informed the magistrates of his intention. The magistrate forbade him to leave the province with the charges unanswered, but there was no attempt to stop him, and the establishment was probably rather relieved. Wesley went first to Charleston, and then boarded a ship bound for England, landing at Deal on 1 February 1738, the day before George Whitefield left for Georgia!

CHAPTER 3

Preaching the new birth

New England

As Wesley and Whitefield struggled in Oxford with their quest for God, events began to unfold on a broader canvas. Jonathan Edwards (1703–58) succeeded his grandfather as pastor of Northampton, Massachusetts, just five years before the extraordinary Awakening or Revival of 1734. There was, of course, a long history of piety in the American colonies. Indeed, as Thomas Kidd has commented, to "expect revival, one had to experience despair, a mood in which the New England Puritans specialized".[1] Many of the ministers, including Solomon Stoddard, Edwards' grandfather, were earnest in their desires. Their gravity was of a particular Puritan and Presbyterian kind. There was a solemn intensity to the pastoral care and exhorting of their congregations. After a dramatic earthquake in 1727 the pastors of New England renewed their call for repentance in the sight of God and the need for a new action of God, an outpouring of the Spirit. This prepared the ground for the events of 1734–35. Edwards sensed that some ministers encouraged laxity among their congregations by suggesting that humanity could contribute towards salvation. Edwards himself was trained and shaped from an early age in prayer. He began to preach on justification by faith alone, and the results were electric. "All seemed to be seized with a deep concern about their eternal salvation," he said in a letter – from the oldest to the youngest, so much so that "no one family that I know of, and scarcely a person, has been exempt".[2] By the spring of 1735 the effect had spread to the surrounding towns in western Massachusetts. Edwards portrayed the event as a great work of God, and described it in his *Faithful Narrative*, published in 1737. He reported individuals coming under intense conviction of sin and crying out because of the burden of their guilt. Weeping was a common accompaniment to conversion. Edwards noted the suddenness, their increasing number, greater awareness of sin, and the fruit of conversion in love, joy, and the praise of God. He was ministering in small, rural towns, settled communities rather than frontier towns. He recorded 600 conversions. The impact was dramatic. We see here the beginnings of the Revival, localized outbreaks which in time were seen as interlinked and not just of local or even national significance, but international.

Conversion

As the Awakening was beginning in Northampton, so Spangenberg had set sail, in January 1735, with his first group of Moravians heading for Georgia. Wesley's years in Georgia were deeply significant; only after he returned to England did he appreciate the full impact of the events in Massachusetts and the influence of his encounter with the Moravians. Their importance for the course of the Revival cannot be underestimated.

Back in Oxford, Whitefield's struggle continued but was nearing its end – so much so that he reported that the Master of Pembroke threatened to expel him for visiting the poor. His tutor was more sympathetic but he described his relatives as alarmed at his change in behaviour. He took counsel from Charles Wesley before the Wesleys' departure for Georgia. Whitefield describes how he felt "great heavings in my body", was unable to sleep, and that God "knows how many nights I have lain upon my bed groaning under the weight I felt... Whole days and weeks have I spent in lying prostrate on the ground."[3] The months went by in fasting and spiritual exercises. Referred by Charles to John, the prescription was more of the same. However, with the Wesleys gone, Whitefield now faced Lent 1735 with the expectations of fasting. The effort made him ill. The moment of conversion was near.

> One day, perceiving an uncommon drought and a disagreeable clamminess in my mouth and using things to allay my thirst, but in vain, it was suggested to me, that when Jesus Christ cried out, "I thirst," His sufferings were near at an end. Upon which I cast myself down on the bed, crying out, "I thirst! I thirst!" Soon after this, I found and felt in myself that I was delivered from the burden that had so heavily oppressed me. The spirit of mourning was taken from me, and I knew what it was truly to rejoice in God my Saviour; and for some time, could not avoid singing psalms wherever I was: but my joy gradually became more settled, and, blessed be God, has abode and increased in my soul, saving a few casual intermissions, ever since.[4]

Whitefield always looked back on this moment, around seven weeks after Easter 1735, as "where Jesus Christ first revealed himself to me and gave me the new birth".[5]

One of the unusual features in the years leading up to the outbreak of Revival was the way in which the future leaders underwent the conversion experience largely independent of each other. When Whitefield received the new birth, Wesley was still in Georgia. Elsewhere, in Wales, a 21-year-old teacher was undergoing a similar experience. Howell Harris (1714–73) was born in the same year as George Whitefield in Trevecca, Breconshire. He became a significant Revival leader, and Trevecca an important place. Harris's upbringing was complicated. In 1730 his brother left for Jamaica and a year later his father died. At the age of just seventeen Harris took a position as a schoolmaster near to his home. His personal and moral behaviour slipped; as his early biographer put it, in a way only an evangelical scribe of a hero of the faith could articulate, "He spent his leisure in the counsel of the wicked and in the seat of the ungodly", a period he later referred to as being in the devil's service.[6] However, as time went on Harris too grew interested in spiritual matters. He was advised to read some of the standard devotional works of the "high church orthodox" and, like Wesley, Whitefield, and others, engaged in fasting, religious exercises, and inner turmoil. His conversion moment came during a service of Holy Communion on 25 May 1735 – receiving assurance of salvation in the grace of God. This was his description:

> At the table, Christ bleeding on the Cross was kept before my eyes constantly; and strength was given me to believe that I was receiving pardon on account of the

blood. I lost my burden; I went home leaping for joy, and I said to my neighbour who was sad, Why are you sad? I know my sins have been forgiven, though I had not heard that such a thing was to be found except in this book. Oh blessed day! Would that I might remember it gratefully evermore![7]

In June 1835, three weeks after his conversion, Harris had a further experience of God while praying and reading Scripture in the tower of Llangasty Church. From this came his zeal for evangelism.

Suddenly I felt my heart melting within me like wax before a fire, and love to God for my Saviour. I felt also not only love and peace, but a longing to die and to be with Christ. Then there came a cry into my soul within that I had never known before – Abba, Father! I could do nothing but call God my Father. I knew that I was His child, and He loved me and was listening to me. My mind was satisfied and I cried out, "Now I am satisfied! Give me strength and I will follow Thee through water and fire."[8]

A month later, another Welshman, Daniel Rowland (1713–90), though already an ordained minister of the Established Church, was also converted, under the guidance of Griffith Jones, an older clergyman with a passion for founding schools, who had some knowledge of the German Pietists. The impact on Rowland's preaching was immediate and astonishing. Mark Noll records a poem by William Williams, after Rowland's death:

Shaking heaven and earth together,
With a voice both strong and new...
Then he sang with gospel charm;
He proclaimed divine salvation.[9]

Just a few years later Howell Harris described remarkable scenes in Rowland's parish of Llangeitho: groans, weepings, joy, scores falling down under the piercing conviction of the word of God.[10] Harris first met Rowland in 1737 in Brecon. Rowland, who was ordained, was a fellow itinerant, and they formed a close friendship which lasted for the next thirteen years until a split divided Welsh Calvinistic Methodism, the association which formed out of revival in Wales. Although the Welsh revivalists sided with Whitefield in the Calvinistic controversies, Harris was a passionate supporter of the Wesleys' attempts at unity and reconciliation. In 1752 he retired to Trevecca and remained loyal to the Established Church, though he also supported the Countess of Huntingdon, who established a training college there in 1768 (see Chapter 6). Harris went up to Oxford in November 1735, but stayed only six weeks. Shocked by the laxity, he returned to Wales. He was denied ordination because of his Methodist views and resolved to remain a layman.

Whitefield, on the other hand, back in Gloucester for several months, had come to the attention of the bishop. To be more precise, the bishop's attention was drawn to Whitefield. He sent for him and told him that he would ordain him when he presented himself for Holy Orders. Looking back in later life, Whitefield told of his struggle at the time with whether he was called and fit for ordination – his *Journal* simply records that "[at] length I came to a resolution, by God's leave, to offer myself for Holy Orders the next Ember Days".[11] Ember Days were the traditional dates for ordinations. Whitefield returned to Oxford and took his public examinations. He was ordained by Bishop Benson of Gloucester on 20 June 1736.

Whitefield's first sermon was on Sunday 27 June 1736 in the Church of St Mary de Crypt in Gloucester. The occasion drew a crowd. He spoke of a heartfelt sense of divine presence. There was a complaint to the bishop! He returned to Oxford and formally took his degree. He stood in as "supply" (that is, he supplied the ministry on a temporary basis) for the curate at the Tower of London for two months, followed, after another spell in Oxford, by ministry in Dummer in Hampshire, near Basingstoke. By this time Charles Wesley was back in England and John Wesley wrote to the Holy Club for more assistance with the work in Georgia. John wrote, "Does your heart not burn within you to turn many others to righteousness?",[12] while Whitefield noted another letter, which asked, "What if thou art the man, Mr Whitefield?"[13] Whitefield described Wesley as his friend (a point that was to be tested), and added that his heart leapt within him and he resolved to respond to the call to Georgia. While he waited to depart he began to preach. He noted during 1737 that he "began to grow a little popular",[14] the congregations were large, and he believed there were conversions. He returned to Bristol. Word spread, congregations grew, and he was invited to preach before the mayor. His themes were the new birth and the doctrine of justification by faith alone in Jesus Christ. He went via Bath and Oxford to London, waiting for Governor Oglethorpe's ship to sail. For three weeks he preached in London and then, with the sailing still delayed, went to Stonehouse in Gloucestershire to supply the ministry. He preached in the church and in the parsonage house and noted that neither "church nor house could contain the people that came".[15] By the end of May, with the supply work in Stonehouse complete, Whitefield accepted invitations to Bristol for a second time. He described listeners hanging onto the rails of the organ loft, people being turned away, and all denominations coming to hear him. He preached again in Bath, collecting £160 for the poor of Georgia. Returning to London he printed his sermon *On the Nature and Necessity of our Regeneration or New Birth*. He preached in numerous London churches – up to nine times a week. He finally left London on board the *Whitaker* on 28 December 1737 and Deal on 2 February 1738. The pace was exhausting.

When Wesley returned to England, much had taken place both personally and more widely. He gave an account to the trustees of the colony on 8 February. Two days earlier he had met Peter Böhler, a Moravian en route to America. Wesley and Böhler met several times between February and May 1738. Wesley was deeply fascinated by the Moravians in Georgia and had corresponded with von Zinzendorf. Böhler talked to Wesley of assurance – which Wesley was prepared to accept – and also of the giving of faith in an instant – which he could not. However, in conversation with others he was directed to many instantaneous conversions in the pages of the Acts of the Apostles. Böhler left on 8 May; on 21 May Charles Wesley experienced conversion, and on Wednesday 24 May 1738 Wesley set out to attend a meeting of Moravians. The journal entry is the famous one.

In the evening I went very unwillingly to a society in Aldersgate Street, where one was reading Luther's Preface to the Epistle to the Romans. About a quarter before nine, while he was describing the change which God works in the heart through faith in Christ, I felt my heart strangely warmed. I felt I did trust in Christ, Christ alone for salvation, and an assurance was given me that he had taken away *my* sins, even *mine*, and saved *me* from the law of sin and death.[16]

Wesley's conversion has functioned as the model. However, as we have noted, it was neither the first nor the only such experience. The building blocks of the conversions of the key players and their early lives and struggles are now in place.

Preaching the new birth at home and abroad

With both their ships still in harbour at Deal, Wesley sent word to Whitefield that the latter should return to London. Whitefield had missed seeing Wesley as John returned to London, but saw no reason to be deterred from his plans, particularly concerned for the colony's pastoral and spiritual welfare. Whitefield sailed into a complex and problematic situation in Georgia. The ship on which he was travelling was transporting soldiers to Georgia to assist in its defence against the Spanish. There were three ships in the convoy, heading to the colonies via Gibraltar. Whitefield was the chaplain, and the task was demanding. He had to engage across the social divides, preside at morning and evening prayers, and catechize and instruct among a less than receptive audience. Many on board the ship, including Whitefield, suffered from seasickness, but he managed to perform a wedding as well as preaching and teaching. He later married a couple on one of the other ships, distributed books and Bibles, and visited the sick – of which there were many. They left Gibraltar on 7 March and on 26 March Whitefield reported the conversion of a young gentleman on board. He also buried the dead, but as he was not in priest's orders he was unable to celebrate Communion on Easter Sunday. On 5 May, a Friday, they at last sighted the Savannah River; two days later they dropped anchor some fourteen miles off Savannah and took a boat to reach the town. Four months later he left Charleston bound again for England.

When Whitefield returned from Georgia he wrote to Howell Harris, news of whom had reached him. He encouraged Harris spiritually and asked him to reply, which he did on 8 January 1739. Harris acknowledged that, though they had not met, he was well aware of Whitefield's ministry. The spiritual outpourings of the letter may seem rather sycophantic, but he reported on the outbreak of revival in various parts of Wales including Carmarthenshire, Breconshire, and Monmouthshire. He mentioned Daniel Rowland, and other ministers supporting the cause, but not by name, as "enemies are many and powerful".[17]

Harris's conversion experience and its aftermath, which we have already described, led to his insatiable need to go and exhort all he met concerning the spiritual state of their souls. Indeed it was this imperative – in a still very young man – that may have contributed to those in authority declining to agree to his ordination in 1736. He began with house-to-house teaching. Ordination was not necessary for such a ministry, but Harris noted that it generated significant opposition in his local parishes:

> At first I knew nothing at all, but God opened my mouth (full of ignorance), filling it with terrors and threatenings. I was given a commission to rend and break sinners in the most dreadful manner. I thundered greatly, denounced the gentry, the carnal clergy and everybody.[18]

The "everybody" probably didn't help his cause. In this admission Harris reveals both the strengths and the weaknesses of the Evangelical Revival, and indeed of "revivalism". He was not uneducated but lacked both formal preparation and call. None of that was to get in the way of a call from God. These were the first outbreaks of Revival and Harris was the first itinerant of the Revival, preceding both Whitefield and Wesley. The power of the commitment to take the gospel message out in the light of the conversion experience meant that many of the early pioneers adopted these methods of itinerancy and open-air preaching. These approaches allowed for larger crowds but the effect was also psychological. The gospel was not to be contained within parish boundaries even if church order sought to preserve the sanctity of those boundaries. The gospel belonged out of doors; there was an imperative to its proclamation. Harris was scathing of the clergy:

> ...Many who wear the cloth... what good they do I know not. Because I led some hundreds of ignorant people to a knowledge of what it means to be

Christians... I am called a madman by those who
claim the office of enlightening the people who are
in darkness.[19]

These events must have given Whitefield much
encouragement. His own early ministry had been well
received. However, the preaching of the new birth was
essentially divisive. The doctrine was not bound by
either geography or ordination. This eventually brought
considerable challenge to the evangelical movement. Neither
parish boundaries nor the laying-on of hands in episcopal
ordination guaranteed salvation. In early February 1739
Whitefield preached in various London churches – St Mary's,
Islington; Wapping Chapel; and St George's-in-the-East – and
received donations for the Savannah Orphan House. More
controversial was his visit to St Margaret's, Westminster, on
4 February. In his *Journal* Whitefield described the mix-up
over preachers as an innocent muddle. Whitefield was guided
to the pulpit by a supporter whom he claimed he took for a
genuine church official. A week later he was in his parish base
in Dummer. He was due to preach in Basingstoke but unable
to do so because of illness, though he did speak to a smaller
crowd. The opposition was becoming clearer. Attempts were
made to stop the proceedings at Basingstoke and a complaint
was made to the bishop; objections were also made to his
preaching in London the previous week. On 14 February
he headed for Bath, and was refused the pulpit of the abbey.
The next day he visited Bristol. He was refused entry to St
Mary Redcliffe and sent packing by the dean, Whitefield in
his *Journal* complaining of the deception used to bar him.
Whitefield did preach to the prisoners in the jail and to a

religious society. He then went, famously, to Kingswood. He reported that "my bowels have long since yearned toward the poor colliers, who are very numerous, and as sheep having no shepherds".[20] The pulpits were closing, the opposition increasing. Yet to Whitefield the need for these poor miners to hear the word of life as he saw it was overwhelming. He would not be prevented by a closed pulpit. He took a momentous step.

> After dinner, therefore, I went upon a mount, and
> spake to as many people as came unto me. There
> were upwards of two hundred. Blessed be God that I
> have now broken the ice! I believe I never was more
> acceptable to my Master than when I was standing
> to teach those hearers in the open fields. Some may
> censure me; but if I thus pleased men, I should not be
> the servant of Christ.[21]

It was a major turning point. Within a month both John and Charles Wesley made the same break with tradition. Over the next few days Whitefield clashed with the Chancellor of the Diocese of Bristol, who threatened to suspend him for preaching without a licence. Then on Wednesday 21 February he returned to Kingswood, this time preaching to nearly 2,000 people. On 4 March there were 4,000 colliers listening to Whitefield's preaching, a few days later 10,000. Whitefield wrote to Wesley urging the brothers to come to Bristol. They were hesitant and in late March John consulted the Fetter Lane Society and (in classic Moravian style, by lot) agreed they should go. In the meantime Whitefield went to Cardiff, met Howell Harris, and then returned to Bristol. On 7 March 1739 he arrived in Cardiff and preached in the town hall to about a hundred hearers. After his sermon he saw Howell Harris approaching him:

> After I came from the seat, I was much refreshed with the sight of my dear brother Howell Harris, whom, though I knew not in person, I have long since loved in the bowels of Jesus Christ.[22]

Whitefield described Harris in glowing terms, and noted that he had twice been refused ordination. Harris, Whitefield added, had founded some thirty religious societies, and spent the last three or four years travelling from place to place (he "has been, I think, in seven counties"). Harris had been courageous in the face of persecution and, Whitefield added, he "discourses generally in a field, but at other times in a house, from a wall, a table or anything else".[23] So here in 1739 we see articulated one of the defining characteristics of the Revival: itinerant preaching. Harris and Whitefield spent the rest of the evening together at an inn, sharing their experiences and taking counsel together. They were clearly drawn to each other and prayed together at the end of the evening.

Wesley's journal entry for 31 March set out his own dilemma:

> In the evening I reached Bristol, and met Mr. Whitefield there. I could scarce reconcile myself at first to this strange way of preaching in the fields, of which he set me an example on Sunday; having been all my life (till very lately) so tenacious of every point

relating to decency and order, that I should have thought the saving of souls almost a sin if it had not been done in a church.[24]

By the Sunday (1 April), with Whitefield heading for Gloucester, Wesley noted in his diary in preaching on the Sermon on the Mount to a religious society that this was an example of field preaching in the ministry of Jesus. The outcome was, by now, probably inevitable. On Monday 2 May he wrote:

At four in the afternoon I submitted to be more vile, and proclaimed in the highways the glad tidings of salvation, speaking from a little eminence in the ground adjoining to the city, to about three thousand people.[25]

Whitefield's ministry continued with visits in and around the Bristol area, together with Bath, Gloucester, and into Wales. The numbers were unquestionably impressive, though it is not clear how they counted the 23,000 reportedly present on Sunday 25 March at Hanham Mount, where many of the colliers lived. A crowd of some size it certainly must have been. He preached to societies and in the open air, was offered church pulpits and denied them, and the pace was nothing short of frantic. He went into Wales in the footsteps of Howell Harris, speaking in meeting rooms, homes, churches, and outside. The ministry was characterized by hymn singing, prayer, and conversation. He challenged the poor at Kingswood and wealthy ladies in Abergavenny. He commented that he "would rather preach the Gospel to the unprejudiced, ignorant colliers, than to the bigoted, self-righteous, formal Christians. The colliers will enter into the

Kingdom of God before them."[26] At Thornbury, denied the pulpit, Whitefield stood on a table and taught in the street.

Whitefield remarked on 25 February at Kingswood that the "fire is kindled in the country; and, I know, all the devils in hell shall not be able to quench it".[27] He corresponded with Wesley in a chatty, friendly manner. He noted "an unhappy clergyman" refusing to share a boat with him at New Passage on the River Severn, received news of the gospel work in Yorkshire under Benjamin Ingham, and was banned from preaching in the prison at Bristol because he proclaimed the new birth. There were reports of people being affected emotionally by the preaching, and often crying. At Cheltenham he referred to some being "so filled with the Holy Ghost that they were almost unable to support themselves under it".[28] His heart, though, was in Georgia, and he hoped that the Lord would bless the ministry of John Wesley, especially among the Kingswood miners. On 31 March Whitefield and Wesley, "my honoured friend", were together. Whitefield, loath to leave Bristol, was consoled only by the knowledge that the colliers would be in Wesley's care. As he put it:

> What gives me the greater comfort is the consideration that my dear and honoured friend, Mr. Wesley, is left behind to confirm those who are awakened, so that, when I return from Georgia, I hope to see many bold soldiers of Jesus Christ.[29]

Whitefield was committed to the Church of England, to the Articles and Homilies that formed part of her foundation documents. He complained that many who had left the

Church of England did so only "because they could not find food for their souls. They stayed among us till they were starved out."[30] He headed to Oxford and by the end of April was in London. The pattern was the same: religious societies, pulpits that were open, private houses, and the open air. He preached at Moorfields and Kennington Common, north and south of the river – 30,000 were estimated to be at Kennington on 29 April. There were many such occasions. Whitefield's own interpretation of the events was that the "Word came with power".[31] He remarked also on the news of Wesley's Bristol ministry. On 27 May he preached to about 20,000 at Moorfields, and the sermon lasted nearly two hours! However, Georgia was calling. Throughout April Wesley remained in Bristol. He preached regularly to the Kingswood miners, to societies, and in and around the city. When a former member of the Holy Club, James Hervey, expressed concern about the open-air preaching, Wesley replied with one of his most famous comments, in a letter of 11 June 1739 (according to his *Works*, but the original date might be earlier):

> I have now no parish of my own, nor probably ever shall... I look upon all the world as my parish... This is the work I know God has called me to do, and I am sure that His blessing attends it.[32]

In London, Charles Wesley was the target of the hostility provoked by John and Whitefield. Even in the sympathetic church of St Mary, Islington, life was made hard for him, with the wardens demanding to see his licence to preach before he could take services as the honorary curate. Charles always had more scruples about breaching church order than either John or George. Whitefield invited Charles to judge for himself and he was astounded by what he saw, bemoaning Whitefield's exclusion from the churches. In April 1739 Whitefield wheeled in Howell Harris to try to persuade Charles, realizing that, with his departure for Georgia, John could not sustain the itinerant ministry alone. Charles still resisted. Towards the end of May Charles accepted an invitation to preach in the church at Broadoaks, Essex. While he was there, a local farmer invited him to preach in his field. He agreed, and preached to 500. He did so again shortly afterwards when the pulpit of Thaxted was closed to his ministry. By the end of June, Charles was preaching at Moorfields.

As with Whitefield, there is some evidence of dramatic events surrounding the preaching: strong cries, tears, and a Quaker who "dropped down as thunderstruck".[33] The next day, "another person reeled four or five steps, and then dropped down".[34] Wesley was clear that, however bizarre the phenomenon, the reality was borne out only by the fruit. His methodical approach was shown in his own organization, with a regular pattern of preaching in particular places on particular days (Monday near Bristol, Tuesday Bath, Wednesday to Saturday in various designated areas of Bristol, then on Sundays four sermons, including to the Kingswood colliers). Every evening Wesley preached to a religious society. In June he was in London, and on 14 June accompanied Whitefield at Blackheath to face a crowd of some 12–14,000 people. Whitefield insisted that Wesley take his place as preacher. That same evening in Wapping, at a religious society, Wesley observed a particularly dramatic outbreak of the phenomena of the Revival – crying, falling down, convulsions, and so on. Wesley returned to Bristol on 18 June. That same evening Howell Harris visited him.

Even in his short absence divisions had broken out in the Bristol society, which Wesley lamented. In July Whitefield was back in Bristol – still awaiting the finalization of his passage to Georgia. Wesley and Whitefield dined together on 10 July, and later that same week they left together for Thornbury. At the end of August Wesley returned to London, about ten days after Whitefield, who had encountered some hostility at Basingstoke while en route. Wesley's preaching continued, not least in Moorfields and Kennington. Whitefield's *Journal* speaks of his preaching to crowds of 20,000 at Newington twice in a week (30 July to 3 August 1739), and 30,000 at Marylebone Fields (1 August). Perhaps illustrating the very personal nature of evangelical faith and the close individual relationships that characterized the Revival, immediately after Marylebone Fields Whitefield went to the Fetter Lane Society – where Wesley had experienced conversion.

As Whitefield had done before him, Wesley asserted his allegiance to the Church of England, its Prayers, Articles, and Homilies, as he put it. The differences with many of the existing clergy did not derive from the fundamental doctrines but rather from their (that is, the unconverted clergy's) understanding of justification as a co-operative enterprise with God and that the new birth was merely an outward sign, rather than an inner revival and transformation of the heart.

By mid-August Whitefield was finally aboard his ship; by the end of October he was in Pennsylvania, on his way to Savannah. Proclaiming new birth did not prevent old disputes from raising their head. Whitefield and Wesley soon began to fall out over matters of doctrine and belief. These disputes both divided and shaped the evangelical movement. The preaching was in the open air and so was the argument.

CHAPTER 4

Dispute and division

The nascent evangelical movement that emerged from the Revival was, within a few years of its birth, sadly divided. For a movement that proclaimed new birth and transformation this was damaging, if not hypocritical. However, for a group that was built on individual salvation, personalities, innovation, and the challenging of established boundaries, the outcome is less surprising. The matters under dispute should also be kept in proportion. There were personality clashes, but for the most part the main protagonists maintained warm personal relationships and held each other in high regard. Wesley and Whitefield constantly sought to keep up a good rapport and to be supportive of each other, and many of the early pioneers retained friendships across the theological divides that emerged. The differences, however, began to come to light very early.

Wesley and the Moravians: Stillness

The central role of the Moravians in the origins of the Revival is incontrovertible, and the personal indebtedness of John Wesley to the Moravian Christians is also difficult to overestimate. The encounter on the way to Georgia in 1735, his connection to Peter Böhler, and, of course, his conversion experience in the Fetter Lane Society of Moravians all contributed to a deep, close, and personal relationship. He admired their piety, worship, community, and organization. Indeed it was the Moravians' methodical approach that inspired Wesley and on which he modelled his Methodist religious societies. In the months immediately after his conversion experience Wesley visited the Moravian Church in Germany. The party arrived in Herrnhut on 1 August 1738. Wesley carefully observed the details of the worship, noting the use of instruments other than the organ, the adoption of extemporary prayer, and the organizational structure of the community. He also interviewed many of the leading members. He left to return to England, via the Pietist centre of Halle, on 11 August.

Inevitably, power as well as religion played a part in the quickly emerging dispute that led to Wesley's separation from the Moravians. To Count Nicholas von Zinzendorf, the Fetter Lane Society was a Moravian outpost; to Wesley, it was one of his religious societies. Theologically the debate was about "faith" and "stillness". The great contribution of the Moravians was to help Wesley understand "faith" as a gift to be received rather than earned or even worked for. However, this could lead to a passivity which was the antithesis of the activism of Methodism.

One aspect of Moravian teaching held that the pathway to true assurance of faith was to exercise stillness or quietness before God until the gift of faith was received. Hence the usual means of grace – the Supper, worship, and prayer – were laid aside until the individual obtained full assurance of faith. Wesley, however, maintained not only that there were degrees of faith but also that the means of grace could be converting and not just confirming ordinances. Wesley, of course, struggled with his own assurance of salvation. There were also other implications. The emphasis on faith meant that good works were downgraded (the classic Catholic argument against Luther's doctrine of justification by faith alone was that it encouraged laziness). This dispute illustrates well how the Moravians were influential on the Revival but not determinative of evangelicalism's settled convictions. Overemphasis on "the wounds of Christ" meant an increased distance between the sinner and the Saviour and reinforced the ideas of stillness and of gazing upon the wounds. Nevertheless, the reclaiming of Luther's doctrine of justification in the Revival meant that the Moravian position appealed to many. Benjamin Ingham, a close associate of Wesley and prominent in the Yorkshire religious societies from the 1740s, continued as an adherent of the Moravians, and he influenced others.

The balloon went up in early 1740. There had already been a power struggle in the Fetter Lane Society between Wesley and Philip Molther. The latter had considerable control on the ground, not least owing to Wesley's absence. In November 1739 Wesley had discovered that members of the Fetter Lane Society were abstaining from good works. They claimed they needed to be "still" before the Lord and denied that they had true faith. He also heard the doctrine preached and advocated at Society meetings. On 15 November, at Bristol, Wesley exhorted the crowds "neither to neglect nor rest in the means of grace",[1] a direct attack on the doctrine of stillness. On 31 November Wesley was in conversation with Molther. He asserted his belief in "degrees of faith" (hence, a person did not need to wait in stillness until they had received the fullness of the gift of faith) and the means of grace (that is, preaching, prayer, and the sacraments). On 19 April 1740 he received a letter urging his return to London owing to the confusion that had now risen to the surface in the Fetter Lane Society. A row had broken out because Charles Wesley, having joint pastoral care of the Society with Molther, had preached on the value of the traditional ordinances. Charles already knew that the future would see a parting. Later in that same week John described a Society meeting as cold, lifeless and lacking brotherly love. In June he preached two sermons to the Society, but on 2 July described their hearts as estranged. Attempts at reconciliation failed. By 18 July the Wesley loyalists had agreed their next step. On Sunday 20 July 1740, John Wesley read a statement to the Fetter Lane Society. He stated that he believed that their assertions that there was no justifying faith without the absence of any doubt and the denial of the means of grace were "flatly contrary to the Word of God", adding that he had borne with them for a long time, but he now had no option but to "give you up to God". His journal entry concluded, "I then, without saying anything more, withdrew, as did eighteen or nineteen of the society."[2] Three days later he noted that their "little company met at *The Foundery*".[3] Wesley's followers had grown in number, and, perhaps in anticipation of future separation, this former cannon factory had been acquired in November 1739 and became a centre for Wesley's operations.

The division was real. The differences were theological but personality and power also played a significant role. The separation of Wesley from the Moravians was probably inevitable and had considerable impact on the Revival's progress. Wesley took what he had learned and experienced, and applied it to his work in England with the Methodist societies. The Moravians were instrumental in the outbreak of Revival, but probably inimical to its advancement. Nevertheless, division and personality differences can also be overplayed. There was a degree of fluidity between the Moravians and the Methodist societies. At different times key players expressed varying degrees of sympathy with the Moravian position – and in later years that included Charles Wesley himself. Faith was certainly a gift, assurance a key part of the Revival doctrine; to Wesley and others, however, it was also an impulse, a gift to be proclaimed and lived out, not simply waited for.

The argument over predestination

The theological dispute that split Wesley and Whitefield was more acute, vicious, and damaging, and infinitely more painful for the participants than the dispute over Moravian stillness. It tore Methodism apart and contributed to its fissure. Some of the impact was long-lasting indeed. One of the biggest casualties was the friendship of Wesley and Whitefield.

A sermon by Wesley, which he preached with little controversy in 1739 and then published in 1740, was the catalyst for the dispute. The key point at issue was the nature of divine election and eternal destiny. In other words, the argument concerned the extent to which the individual was chosen by God for eternal salvation or eternal damnation. Did God select, or elect, individuals for salvation or damnation from the beginning, or did people have the free will to respond to the message? Whitefield took the former line, Wesley the latter. This in turn led to a further question:

if God chose those to be saved, did Christ die only for them (the elect) rather than for everybody? Was the atonement universal or limited? If Christ's death was effective only for the elect, what did this say about the efficacy of preaching? There was also the danger of antinomianism (that is, since the elect will be saved, there is no need for the chosen to live a disciplined, holy life). These arguments were not new. The alternative views derived from the Reformation disputes between followers of John Calvin (1509–64) and Jacob Arminius (1560–1609).

The extent to which Whitefield embraced these Calvinistic doctrines prior to 1740 is a matter of debate. Two things are clear. First, he was generally sympathetic to the Calvinist position before 1740 but in a moderate fashion. This is perhaps not entirely surprising, as he did after all have the Church of England's Articles of Religion (1571) on his side. Article 17 of the Church of England's confessional document aligned the Church explicitly with the Calvinist view on predestination. Wesley too, of course, read the Articles, but unlike Whitefield he was more explicitly influenced by the high-church holiness quest of William Law, which was definitely not Calvinist. Second, Whitefield's views hardened after his encounters with Calvinist ministers in the American colonies in the period 1739–41.

The friendship and genuine love between Wesley and Whitefield was such that the latter left his Bristol societies and work in the former's care when he went to London in 1739 to prepare for his return to the American colonies. Whitefield had urged Wesley not to enter into controversies or disputes, especially as the doctrine was so well ingrained. Wesley did not follow his advice. Whether he meant to cause trouble or not, the impact was unmistakable. Yet the initial sermon, preached on 29 April 1739 under the title "Free Grace" to a crowd of some 4,000 people, was not initially controversial. The occasion is noted in his *Journal*, but only in passing, Wesley concentrating as usual on his schedule of preaching and the response of the hearers. Noteworthy also is that in Whitefield's journal entry for the very next day, Monday 30 April, he referred to having heard of "the wonderful success of my honoured friend Mr. John Wesley's ministry in Bristol".[4] All too often it is the later adherents of competing positions who rather too easily see the division between their heroes. However, Wesley was determined to oppose the doctrine of predestination. He described himself as being led to speak strongly and explicitly on it. In order to confirm what he should do, rather bizarrely he cast a lot – a practice he had observed at Herrnhut, and which he adopted on a number of occasions. The result of the lot was "preach and print", as Whitefield put it in a letter of December 1740. Wesley viewed himself as preaching against extreme Calvinism, believing that it was not possible to hold to lesser degrees of the terrible doctrines – in other words, it was all or nothing: either God chose us for salvation or damnation, or we chose him. This was the opposite of the position that Wesley held in respect of the Moravian view on justification. Whitefield pointed out that not all held the extreme form of the doctrines. In any event, correspondence ensued. Whitefield and Wesley were together in London in June on positive and friendly terms, as noted earlier. Wesley's printer, James Hutton, had refused to print the sermon because he disagreed with it and it seems that Wesley held back for a while. Whitefield wrote to Wesley in June urging silence on both sides, noting that it was already in the public domain "that there is a division between you and me".[5] He also reported that his heart was grieved at any such disagreement. In early July Whitefield pleaded with Wesley not to print the sermon for the sake of peace: "If you have any regard for the peace of the church, keep in your sermon on predestination."[6] Wesley published in August 1739.

With Whitefield heading for the colonies, there was a chance the controversy would die down. However, in America he became more Calvinist, and Wesley in England was not going to give way. Arriving in Philadelphia, Whitefield was quickly in demand for preaching – both inside and outside churches – for counsel among the ministers, and for personal spiritual direction. As usual the state of the clergy did not escape his strictures: the generality of those of the Church of England, he bemoaned, "do not preach or live up to the truth as it is in Jesus".[7] Whitefield made the acquaintance of a leading Presbyterian minister, Gilbert Tennent, and corresponded with Jonathan Edwards. His relationships were now reaching far beyond the ranks of the Church of England. In Charleston, South Carolina, he preached in a dissenters' meeting house and, on 10 January 1740, he was in Savannah, Georgia. Correspondence with Wesley continued, several letters crossing in the post. In one letter dated 26 March 1740 Whitefield referred to Wesley as his honoured friend and brother and rejoiced in the work done at his hands. The doctrine of election, he wrote, "I am ten thousand times more convinced of, if possible, than when I saw you last."[8] The prospects for reconciliation were fading.

In his preaching and writing Whitefield gave ever greater weight to his Calvinist thinking – which he claimed he believed because it was the teaching of Christ, not just of Calvin. He caused scandal among Anglican clergy when he referred to Gilbert Tennent as a faithful minister of Jesus Christ and confirmed he had led a Communion service in a Baptist chapel and was willing to receive the bread and wine of Communion from a Baptist minister. Whitefield asked Wesley not to continue the disputation for fear of it damaging their brotherly love. He lamented Luther's disputes with Zwingli, which had dominated the latter part of his life, and agreed they should "offer salvation freely to all by the blood of Jesus".[9] Indeed, Whitefield's statement shows that many of the attacks from Wesley were aimed at a straw person; both agreed on the proclamation of the new birth; they differed over the origin of and response to the message. Whitefield pleaded with Wesley in a letter of June 1740, "For Christ's sake, if possible, never speak against election in your sermons... For Christ's sake let us not be divided amongst ourselves. Nothing so much will prevent a division as your being silent on this hand."[10] Perhaps something was getting through to Wesley. In August he said to Whitefield that there were bigots on both sides but, although they now differed, in time God would make them of one mind. Both Whitefield and Wesley were equally convinced whose mind it was to which the other would be conformed!

Wesley had some difficulties at home on the matter and this correspondence continued while he was in dispute with the Fetter Lane Society over "stillness". Predestination was not the only area of contention. Wesley had more difficulty explaining to a much wider audience his views on "Christian perfection" than he did his beliefs about predestination. In essence he believed it possible for the convert to live a life free from sin. There was much dispute over language and meaning, interpretation and misinterpretation. Wesley insisted that his main point was that Christian perfection implied the dedication of the whole heart to Christ; there were certainly others who interpreted his claims as implying a cleansing from sin and a life on earth without the daily struggle. This debate continued throughout the Revival, but it was predestination that caused the break. Wesley, after all, had "cast his lot". After he had the sermon printed and distributed, his brother Charles entered the fray, congratulating John and publishing some hymns emphasizing the offer of free grace to *all*. Hymnody too became a battleground. Whitefield later objected, with some justification, that Wesley had promised not to dispute on matters of disagreement but then published his sermon at home and abroad, and Charles wrote hymns to accompany it! Whitefield wrote on 24 December 1740:

> God only knows, what unspeakable sorrow of heart I have felt on your account, since I left England last. Whether it be my infirmity or not, I frankly confess, that Jonah could not go with more reluctance against Nineveh, than I now take pen in hand to write against you.[11]

It was a long letter. Whitefield queried Wesley's reliance on the lot. The latter's choice of text, Romans 8, drew some irony from Whitefield: had "any one a mind to prove the doctrine of *election*, as well as of *final perseverance*, he could hardly wish for a text more fit for his purpose, than that which you have chosen to disprove it".[12] He declared himself more than ever convinced about election and accused Wesley of being illogical. What is more, both Scripture and Article 17 of the

Thirty-nine Articles were against Wesley. Wesley had claimed that the doctrine rendered preaching useless – this was surely a false accusation to bring against Whitefield, of all people, who responded that preaching was God's appointed means of grace to be the power of God for salvation. Similarly, election and predestination encouraged holiness among the followers of Jesus – how else would his true disciples live? – rather than laziness. Wesley pointed out that with predestination people faced eternal damnation through no fault of their own. Whitefield contested only the second part of the assertion with reference to the doctrine of original sin. He finished by looking forward to Wesley's conversion to his point of view, shrouded, of course, in pietistic language:

> There, I am persuaded, I shall see dear Mr. Wesley convinced of election and everlasting love. And it often fills me with pleasure, to think how I shall behold your casting your crown down at the feet of the Lamb, and as it were filled with a holy blushing for opposing the divine sovereignty in the manner you have done.
>
> But I hope the Lord will shew you this before you go hence. O how do I long for that day! If the Lord should be pleased to make use of this letter for that purpose, it would abundantly rejoice the heart of, dear and honoured Sir… George Whitefield.[13]

The divide was complete. When Whitefield returned to England, Wesley resolved to see him and they met on 28 March 1741. Wesley's *Journal* records that he wanted to see him to allow Whitefield to speak for himself. The outcome was not pretty.

He told me he and I preached two different gospels, and therefore he not only would not join with, or give me the right hand of fellowship, but was resolved publicly to preach against me and my brother, wheresoever he preached at all.[14]

How far these evangelicals had come, and in so short a time. There were attempts at reconciliation in subsequent years, with concessions, correspondence, occasional meetings, and preaching for each other and on occasion together. Whitefield claimed he would not see Wesley in heaven, because Wesley would be so near to the throne. In his will Whitefield requested that Wesley preach the funeral sermon (in fact he preached a memorial sermon in London, as Whitefield died in the American colonies).

Varieties of Methodism and its organization

Ultimately these divisions became entrenched. Individual groups chose to position themselves in particular ways. In 1741 John Cennick led around fifty members of Wesley's Methodist group in Bristol into association with Whitefield. Most of the regular Anglican evangelical clergy were by conviction and disposition moderate Calvinists. Many sympathized with Whitefield, but in essence wished to remain part of the Established Church. Others were more sympathetic to Wesley, who was by far the better organized. Through his societies Wesley had a ready-made organizational structure for his developing band of lay preachers and other adherents. Methodism was still a method within the Established Church, and only later did it develop into a separate denomination.

The term "Methodist", certainly in the early decades of the Revival, covered all varieties of evangelical from Wesley to Whitefield to Howell Harris, the regular Anglican clergy such as William Grimshaw and Samuel Walker, and, of course, the Countess of Huntingdon. Wesley began to establish meeting houses for his lay itinerants to preach in, yet he continued to both practise and urge attendance at the parish church alongside the meetings of the societies. Whitefield's regular absence due to visits to the colonies seriously affected his own organizational success. Wesley was especially gifted at this and gave it his full attention, with long-term results.

Calvinism was also organizing. Some of the religious societies were specifically linked to Whitefield, and his own organizational base was his tabernacle (place of worship) in Moorfields, established in 1741. The itinerants and societies were divided into four associations. On 7 January 1742, two years before the first Methodist Conference, the Welsh Methodists gathered together under the chairmanship of Daniel Rowland. There were some twenty others in attendance, including Howell Harris. Whitefield was invited to the Welsh conference and wrote with his advice. Strikingly, he remarked that "some of you are ministers of the Church of England, but if faithful I cannot think you will continue in it long. However, do not go out till you are cast out... be not afraid to preach in the fields."[15] Again there is a pattern of loyalty, preparation, and realism. The Welsh Methodists desperately wanted Whitefield's counsel; there was already tension between Rowland and Harris. A further conference was arranged to enable Whitefield to attend. On 5 and 6 January 1743 eight men, four ordained and four lay, met under Whitefield's watchful gaze at Waterford in South

Wales. Detailed rules were drawn up and plans laid for local monthly conferences, and quarterly and annual meetings. Three months later, on 6 and 7 April, the same eight met again and formed the Calvinistic Methodist Association, with Whitefield as life moderator and Howell Harris appointed to act in his absence. It was a full eighteen months before Wesley called together his Conference.

This Conference, another significant milestone, had its origins in the gathering together in 1744 by John and Charles Wesley of four other Anglican clergy (John Hodges, Henry Piers, John Meriton, and Samuel Taylor) and four itinerant preachers. This became the annual Methodist Conference. The first Conference met at the Foundry to enquire into the spiritual state of the societies. The minutes set down some spiritual standards, carefully distinguishing Wesleyan Methodism from its rivals. The plan was to organize into societies and bands – that is, small groups – but not to separate from the Church of England. Lay preachers were accorded equal status with the ordained, and given their assignments. To some this amounted to insurrection, to others it was a renewal movement. In reality it was both. The organization was nothing if not methodical. The leadership clearly rested with John Wesley. In the gathering of lay itinerants, the formation of small groups for spiritual edification, and its national reach, Methodism was established as a society within a church, which was where Wesley intended it to remain. When that was no longer possible, the structure was in place for Methodism to become a church in its own right. That, however, lay in the future. Organization was an important factor in the success of Methodism but did not lie at its heart. Mark Noll's survey of the rise and development of evangelicalism powerfully asserts the real reasons for the expansion of Wesleyan Methodism:

> It was not primarily organisation but activity, not primarily structure but zeal, not primarily order but sacrifice that made this Methodism a marvel of Christian energy.[16]

Wesley rode the length and breadth of the land. Wesleyan Methodism reached both the poor and unbelievers more generally in ways in which neither the Established Church nor traditional dissent succeeded in doing – the lay itinerants and local societies perhaps being most significant in this development. The movement was not without tensions. Once Methodism became established it took on many establishment features; the poor felt marginalized again, and there emerged yet another dissenting movement, the Primitive Methodists, but that is really beyond our story.

In 1744 Whitefield, with his wife (he had married Elizabeth in 1741), left again for the American colonies and on this occasion did not return until 1748. At home Wesley was active. He travelled some 250,000 miles in total, and never fewer than 4,500 miles a year. He rose at 5 a.m., preached at 6 a.m., and travelled some sixty miles a day to speak at two or three more places. In the winter months he based himself in London or Bristol. The rest of the year he concentrated his efforts on key places from Cornwall to Staffordshire, Yorkshire, Teesdale, and Weardale. Like Whitefield he preached to large crowds, in the West Country most famously at Gwennap Pit. However, Wesley worked mostly through the individual societies, groups of workers, and repeat visits, and in this way, unlike Whitefield, he built a lasting legacy.

CHAPTER 5

Spreading the flame: The early pioneers

The story of the Revival is one of dynamic intensity of spiritual experience, idiosyncratic individuals, innovation, conflict, and the remarkably inexplicable. The characters and stories of the Wesleys and Whitefield shine through, but they were not alone. Since several individuals experienced the new birth at a similar time in various places, the impact was countrywide. These early pioneers, from the 1740s onwards, played a crucial role in bringing the Revival to various communities and indeed in how the phenomenon itself was understood. The crucial first step was usually that of open-air, field preaching, followed by itinerancy, with all the associated tensions within the Established Church.

William Grimshaw of Haworth

The parish of Haworth, set among the rugged hills and steep valleys of Yorkshire, is a mere ten miles from Bradford. Today the village is best remembered for its connections with the Brontë family. Patrick Brontë, born in 1802, was minister of Haworth from 1820 to 1861. Patrick was an evangelical; the family fame derives mainly from his daughters' literary output.

William Grimshaw was born nearly one hundred years before Patrick Brontë, on or about 14 September 1708 (there is some confusion over the actual date) in the village of Brindle, six miles south of Preston in Lancashire. Grimshaw would, in time, experience evangelical conversion, adopt Methodist methods, and, like the Wesleys, remain firmly committed to ministry within the Established Church, although not necessarily within its parochial boundaries. Grimshaw was minister of Haworth from 1742 until his death in 1763. He formed a deep and lasting friendship with both the Wesleys and Whitefield, all of whom preached regularly in Haworth. Grimshaw showed a distinct ability to rise above the theological disputes that divided the two better-known evangelists. He was Wesley's nominated successor and named as such by Wesley's Conference. He itinerated – travelling from place to place with the message of the gospel – while seeking to remain generally within the expectations of the Established Church. He baulked at proposals to permit lay preachers to preside over the sacrament of the Supper. He was a hero to some and "mad Grimshaw" to others. He generated opposition from other clergy, negotiated his way around archbishops, and suffered immense personal tragedy during his ministry, with the successive deaths of two wives and one daughter. His greatest concern was for the spiritual welfare of those in his care, and he was as much at home speaking to a small group in a cottage as standing alongside Whitefield on a specially made platform preaching to thousands in the churchyard.

Henry Venn (see Chapter 7), who preached Grimshaw's funeral sermon, recorded both the verdict of the faithful

— "witness, ye moors and mountains, how often he was in perils by the way, whilst carrying the glad tidings of salvation to some company of poor cottagers…" — and the genuine hardship Grimshaw faced: "in this work, no roads were too dangerous, no refreshment too coarse, no lodging too hard, no discouragement too great".[1]

Grimshaw had had little religious influence on his upbringing. He entered Cambridge in 1726 as a sizar – similar to the servitor role that George Whitefield took at Oxford. A year later he gained a scholarship. However, Grimshaw fell into the dissolute ways that so bedevilled Oxford and Cambridge in this period – though of course those who later recounted the story with the hindsight of providence were keen to note his sins, as it made the conversion story all the more effective. Henry Venn noted the observations of a friend: "Bad example deplorably prevailed to seduce him."[2] He graduated in 1730 with little academic distinction and, unshaken by such matters as faith or lifestyle, sought an appointment as a curate. Ordination was a common career path with minimal requirements of spiritual vitality. Grimshaw was ordained in 1732 as curate to the Vicar of Rochdale. Through this period he oscillated between a quest for seriousness – encouraged by the fact that he had accepted ordination – and his perhaps more natural inclination to succumb to temptation and a carefree lifestyle. For a time he was linked with a group in Rochdale who met weekly for prayer and spiritual nourishment. Alas for Grimshaw, this was not to last, for he soon moved to Todmorden, nestling in the hills between Lancashire and Yorkshire, part of the same parish but more distant from the centres of population, as it lay some eight miles from Halifax. In 1735 he married Sarah

Sutcliffe, a widow two years his junior. Her family home, Ewood Hall, became a centre for Methodism and was visited regularly by the Countess of Huntingdon. Sarah presented William with a son, John, in April 1736. Eleven months later, Jane was born. Tragedy would come later; John was the only survivor of this first family and was a disappointment. Grimshaw went through periods of seriousness again as he sought a salvation that involved looking for God with ever greater earnestness and living a good life in order to please him. No details are known of the tragic illness that befell Sarah, but on 1 November 1739, at the age of twenty-nine, she died, leaving her husband, curate of Todmorden, with two children under five years old to care for. Grimshaw was just thirty-one. Inevitably he faced many troughs, depressions, and internal conflicts.

The evangelical conversion experience is seldom as sudden as in its later retelling. So it was with Grimshaw. In the midst of his mental anguish he picked up a book from a friend's table – the Puritan John Owen on *The Doctrine of Justification by Faith*. Grimshaw told Henry Venn that he was now ready to "embrace Christ only for my all in all", and "O what light and comfort did I now enjoy in my own soul and what a taste of the pardoning love of God".[3] Again he experienced something of a spiritual renaissance. In 1741 he married again, though his new bride, Elizabeth, showed little sympathy for his spiritual work. Seeking fresh pastures for his new wife and his two children, Grimshaw applied to be appointed minister of Haworth in the spring of 1742. Perhaps a sign of things to come, the appointment was not straightforward. Grimshaw's predecessor, Isaac Smith, had been removed by the Ecclesiastical Courts. The appointment was under the control of the Vicar of Bradford, who, possibly aware of Grimshaw's renewed solemnity, refused to appoint him. However, the funding for the post (officially that of a "chapelry") came from the rents of four local farms. The trustees of the farms preferred Grimshaw, and they had the power to either pay or withhold the stipend. Each party sought to protect their rights in the Ecclesiastical Courts, but in the end Grimshaw was appointed.

Grimshaw's conversion

Grimshaw's spiritual state was confused; he sought to be a faithful minister, orthodox in belief, taking seriously the nature of the office he occupied. He was, however, continually buffeted by doubt, temptation, and emotional turmoil. He lacked the assurance of faith that came with the evangelical conversion. He was, however, slowly coming into contact with other early Revival preachers. In 1743 he met Benjamin Ingham – who had been a member of Wesley's Holy Club – and then in 1744 he heard, with some concern, about the presence in the area of William Darney, a maverick revivalist preacher known as "Scotch Will". He was determined to listen to Darney first-hand, rather than go by his innate suspicions. When Grimshaw recognized the message as consistent with his own beliefs, the unlikely pair struck up a friendship. In August of that year Grimshaw made his second covenant with God – a sort of spiritual agreement. The first had been in 1738 as part of his "quest for seriousness". He made yet another covenant in 1752, in which he stated, "Once more and for ever, I most solemnly give up, devote and resign all I am, spirit, soul and body, to thee, and to thy pleasure and command, in Christ Jesus my Saviour." He also looked back:

> Thou knowest, O Lord, I solemnly covenanted with
> thee, in the year 1738; and before that wonderful
> manifestation of thyself unto me, at church, and in the
> clerk's house, between the hours of ten and two o'clock
> on Sunday, September 2, 1744...[4]

The incident to which Grimshaw referred (the manifestation of God) was recounted two years later to Joseph Williams, a merchant from Kidderminster. Subsequently, John Newton, a friend from 1758, also retold the story, visited Haworth, and obtained various details from Grimshaw's maid. The servant reported that on the Sunday in question she had found her master at prayer as early as 5 a.m. Apparently having not eaten anything, Grimshaw collapsed at the reading desk during the morning service. He was escorted to the local inn near the church, dizzy, disorientated, and

> under some apprehension that this seizure might
> issue in death, he all the way through the church
> and churchyard to the clerk's house very earnestly
> exhorted the people to prepare to die; to be always
> ready to fly to Christ and to abide in him; to trust in
> him only for salvation etc.[5]

His limbs were icy cold. He was in some sort of trance for an hour. A friend reported on Grimshaw's experience:

> He thought he saw as it were a dark foul passage into
> which he must go: & being entered, saw on the right
> hand a great high wall on the other side which was
> Heaven, & another on the left on the other side which

was Hell. He overheard God the Father holding a conference with the Lord Jesus Christ concerning him, & for a long time it seemed to go very hard with him, for God the Father would have him to be doomed because he had not wholly relinquished his own righteousness to trust solely and entirely in the merits & righteousness of Christ: but the Lord Jesus pleaded for him. When he had been held in suspense a long time, hoping yet fearing, at last he evidently [i.e. clearly] saw the Lord Jesus thrust down His hands & feet, as it were thro' the ceiling, whilst he particularly observed the wounds in them, & observed the nail-holes to be ragged & bluish, & fresh blood streaming from each of them.[6]

Williams reported that Grimshaw was instantly filled with joy and the circulation returned to his legs. He began the next church service at 2 p.m., apparently not dismissing the congregation until 7 p.m. Some scholars view this incident as conversion; others think that it represented his acceptance of full assurance of salvation. In any event, Grimshaw was transformed.

Grimshaw's ministry
Haworth brought spiritual challenges from the beginning. Life was tough, and the spiritual input over the years had been modest. Funerals often descended into drunkenness, the Sunday market in Bradford was infinitely more attractive than the pulpit of the parish church, and Sunday sport involved football on the moors. This was the situation Grimshaw faced. However, he had high expectations of his parishioners'

attendance at divine service. He would stroll across the moors to track down the footballers. He once disguised himself in order to join some youthful local revellers in a well-known gathering place. When he was finally recognized the youths fled in some panic! Another time he shamed a parishioner's miserly attitude towards those in need by dressing as a beggar and appearing at his door. There are numerous other stories, some of which are apocryphal. John Newton reported that Grimshaw frequently left the church during the singing of the psalm before the sermon to round up idlers in the churchyard and revellers at the inn.[7] However, the suggestion that it was all 176 verses of Psalm 119 that were sung and that he used a horsewhip may be an embellishment. Grimshaw was spiritually passionate and that drove him in unusual ways and directions; in the context of the Revival, they were at least more understandable.

Grimshaw's methods were classically Methodist. He formed classes and small groups and as time went on made use of lay assistants. In a 1747 letter to John Wesley, Grimshaw reported his practice of "monthly visitation" – that is, of gathering eight to ten families together in dwelling places scattered around his parish for teaching and exhortation. In 1747 he reported to Archbishop Hutton that on his arrival in Haworth there were twelve communicants. In 1743, one year after his institution, the then Archbishop of York, Thomas Herring, conducted a visitation of his diocese. Grimshaw reported to him that there were 326 families, two services each Sunday, and five Communions per year at which there were around fifty to sixty communicants – already some significant growth. The importance of Grimshaw's ministry, however, really emerged after his conversion experience in 1744.

A significant feature of early Methodism was itinerancy. Within the Church of England, where most of the early pioneers operated, this was frowned on at best and thoroughly opposed by many. The Church of England was built upon its parish system and the geographical boundaries of the structure were policed by the local clergy. In theory the arrangement provided for ministry to each and every parish. The question that the early evangelicals faced was what to do if the gospel of new birth was not being proclaimed.

By 1746 the effects of the ministry in Haworth were beginning to be felt in neighbouring parishes. Many flocked to hear Grimshaw and so the invitations came to preach the message elsewhere, often in private homes or barns. This provoked the ire of the parish clergy concerned. The same year brought more personal tragedy, with his second wife, Elizabeth, dying from a fever. Charles Wesley noted in his *Journal* that she had at first opposed her husband's spiritual work, but lately was convinced.[8] In January 1747 Grimshaw entertained Charles Wesley at Haworth but was exercised by the possible implications of the invitation. His hesitation was short-lived and he opened his pulpit from this point on to the Wesleys and to George Whitefield and other evangelical leaders. His fears overcome, he wrote to Wesley on 20 August 1747 describing his "Nicodemical fear" and the offence caused to the clergy, "which, till lately almost made me ready to sally out no more, but to content myself in my own bounds". However, he also referred to his mind being "deeply affected with strong impressions to preach the gospel abroad", and "fearing to be disobedient to what I trust was the heavenly call".[9] The work quickly expanded, as did the workload – he wrote to Wesley pleading for assistance.

Grimshaw clashed particularly with George White, the Vicar of Colne, and Benjamin Kennet, technically his own vicar. His accusers brought charges against him before the new Archbishop of York, Matthew Hutton, in May 1748. Grimshaw responded to the archbishop's questions on the number of communicants by reporting that the numbers had risen from twelve when he arrived to four or five hundred and nearer twelve hundred in the summer. Hutton declared he could find no fault with him. From this point on Grimshaw began to itinerate regularly on what became known as "the great Haworth round". Writing to Wesley, he described his itinerary over the course of five days from Chester to the Pennine villages and Sheffield, visiting societies and welcomed by sympathetic clergy. These "circuits" were designed so that Grimshaw could return to his own parish for Sundays so as not to neglect his own parishioners.

After John Wesley's first visit to Haworth, Grimshaw wrote to him and declared that his "pulpit, I hope, shall be always at yours and your brother's service; and my house, so long as I have one, your welcome home".[10] In May 1747 Wesley recorded in his diary that he had "read prayers and preached in Haworth church to a numerous congregation".[11] Wesley visited again in August 1748, followed by George Whitefield's first visit in September of the same year. Wesley and Grimshaw got into something of a scrap with the constable of nearby Barrowford – Wesley was beaten to the ground and then the mob "threw Mr Grimshaw down and loaded them both with dirt and mire of every kind",[12] the constable declining to intervene to protect the victims.

Grimshaw, a widower once again, now made alternative arrangements for his children's schooling, sending them to Wesley's school in Kingswood, Bristol. Whitefield had landed from America in July 1748 and visited Haworth in the September. Part of Whitefield's *Journal* has been lost, but an early biographer quoted from it, noting, "in the parish church where this venerable apostle constantly laboured, I administered the Lord's Supper to upwards of a thousand communicants, and preached in the church-yard to six thousand hearers",[13] numbers confirmed by Whitefield's extant correspondence.[14] Whitefield was back in 1749 and 1750; the pattern was the same, preaching in the church, administering the sacrament at a second service, and then addressing thousands in the churchyard. None of this protected Grimshaw from further tragedy; his daughter Jane died in 1750 at Kingswood at the age of twelve. Whitefield visited again in 1752. "Thousands upon thousands have flocked twice and thrice a day to hear the word of life," he said in his visits to Birstall, Haworth, and Halifax.[15] In 1752 it was Charles Wesley's turn to visit. Charles had comforted William after Jane's death. He reported that he preached to three or four thousand in Haworth and then a second time to double that number. In 1753, it was Whitefield again. John Wesley also visited in 1752 and 1753. Then in 1755 Wesley noted in his *Journal* that he had been "obliged to go out of the church, abundance of people not being able to get in".[16] The rain also providentially ceased for Wesley to preach.

That same year work began on extending the church – Whitefield preached in the new church in October 1755. The problem of preaching to thousands of people remained, and in 1756 a more expedient method was found: a scaffolding pulpit which would enable the preacher to pass through a window from the inside of the church onto a scaffold platform on the outside, and so preach to the crowds. Whitefield was the first to use it in 1756. The visits of both Wesleys and Whitefield continued on a regular basis. Wesley recorded in his *Journal* on 22 May 1757:

> A storm met us on the mountain, but this did not hinder
> such a congregation as the church could not contain.
> I suppose we had near a thousand communicants, and
> scarce a trifler among them. In the afternoon the church
> not containing more than a third of the people, I was
> constrained to be in the churchyard.[17]

This time the rain did not stop. Two years later, on 22 July 1759, he added:

> The church would not near contain the congregation; so
> after prayers I stood on a scaffold close to the church,
> and the congregation in the churchyard.[18]

And, on 12 July 1761:

> The church would not near contain the people;
> however, Mr Grimshaw had provided for this by
> fixing a scaffold on the outside of one of the windows,
> through which I went after prayers, and the people
> likewise all sent out into the churchyard. The afternoon
> congregation was larger still. What has God wrought in
> the midst of these rough mountains.[19]

Grimshaw was a tough northerner. He dealt with the reality of people's lives, not least their spiritual destiny. Indeed, he was so focused on the idea of eternal salvation and the urgency of the message that he was more than capable of rebuking his guest speakers. John Newton records on one occasion that Grimshaw interrupted George Whitefield in the pulpit as he was commenting on the privileges they enjoyed in Haworth: "For God's sake do not speak so. I pray you do not flatter them. The greater part of them are going to Hell with their eyes open."[20]

All this took its toll on Grimshaw's health. He once described preaching as his health and food and physic, although we do not have the original text: "O that we may spend and be spent in preaching His everlasting gospel, in converting sinners and confirming believers."[21]

Grimshaw was fifty-four years old when he died. His health had deteriorated rapidly, and fever and epidemic were ever-present realities in Haworth. One such epidemic broke out in early 1763. Already weak, he insisted on visiting the sick. Perhaps it was inevitable that he would fall ill with the fever, which he did around 20 March. He made his will and funeral arrangements. By 7 April he was dead.

Assessment

One of Grimshaw's early biographers, William Myles in 1806, included a reprint of some of his writings. Acknowledging that we do not have the original, the following extract helps us in assessing his importance:

> What a dangerous mistake those people are under, who believe and are taught as the *modern language* of but too many of *our pulpits,* that *conversion* is nothing more than a turning from a *bad* to a *good* life, and that if they do

their best, striving to *live as well as they can,* the Lord
will forgive their sins and save their souls. This notion
or doctrine... is utterly contrary to the Holy Bible,
39 Articles, Catechism and Liturgy of the Church of
England, and the *principles of our dissenting brethren.*[22]

Revival has perhaps fared best in frontier situations. In
England this was seen in the flourishing of Methodism in the
Pennines and in Cornwall. Grimshaw was certainly a pioneer.
He illustrates for historians some fascinating characteristics.
First, it is essential to recognize the centrality and vitality of
the Revival within the Church of England. Capitalizing on
the word "Methodist" can disguise the fact that no separate
denomination existed at this time and many "Methodists"
worshipped in the parish churches and also met together in
their classes, societies, and bands. Second, Grimshaw showed
a firm grasp of the classic reformed doctrine of justification
by faith alone – that is, that salvation comes through faith
in Christ alone rather than by living a good life. This is an
important element of continuity from the Reformation.
Third, he was clear that the true Church of England, as
reflected in its formularies and liturgy, adopted this doctrinal
position. Hence not only is there no point in departing from
the Church, because of its opportunities, parochial provision,
and so on, but there are many advantages in being part of
the Established Church. Fourth, unity in Christ means co-
operation across denominational boundaries because of
shared belief and doctrine.

These points reflect the basic tenets of the early pioneers.
Grimshaw's importance, however, goes further. Like
Whitefield, he was a moderate Calvinist, believing in God's

predestination of those he will save rather than accepting Wesley's emphasis on free will. Like Whitefield, he rejected the Wesleyan doctrine of the possibility of Christian perfection. However, driven by his pioneering ministry and by the preaching of the new birth, he remained the closest of friends with both John and Charles Wesley and George Whitefield, who were often in some degree of dispute. Grimshaw's moderate adoption of "extraordinary measures", his co-operation across denominational lines, his adherence to the Established Church, and his unity of purpose and friendship with the Wesleys and Whitefield are a mark of his significant role and contribution.

Samuel Walker of Truro

J. C. Ryle, the evangelical Bishop of Liverpool from 1880 to 1900, said, "I venture the surmise that in the last day, when the secrets of all ministries shall be disclosed, few will be found to have done better work for Christ in their day and generation than Walker of Truro."[23] Ryle had earlier commented that "he was one who cultivated his own corner of the Lord's vineyard with such singular success, that there were few places in England, where such striking results could be shown from preaching the gospel as at Truro".[24] G. R. Balleine claimed that the "work that he accomplished was extraordinary".[25] Walker, like Grimshaw, reflects many of the themes of the Revival and yet his conclusions, in a number of respects, were quite different. Walker's ministry represented the faithful exercise of pastoral ministry by an evangelical convert of the Church of England in many years of labour within his own parish. His spirituality was identical to that of Whitefield and Grimshaw – in other words, he was a moderate Calvinist. So was his labour – he was worn out by his exertions, dying on 19 July 1761 at the age of forty-six. However, he resisted itinerancy, opposed the adoption of lay ministry, was reluctant in his support of Methodist societies, and had a rather edgy relationship with John Wesley. In all these things he was most unlike William Grimshaw. So Walker illustrates for us another type of pioneer.

Cornwall, like Yorkshire, might be described as pioneer country. Arguably more remote, even marginal, its people too expressed a rugged independence and individualism. Tin mining was the main legal industry, smuggling the illegal – the participants were often the same people. The county was poor and the problems of drink were never far from the surface. Cornwall became a focus of the Revival, among evangelical clergy of the Church of England, in the development of Methodist societies under Wesley's influence and control, and later for Methodism as a denomination. Relationships between the two strands were, at times, tense.

There was nothing particularly unusual about Samuel Walker in the context of eighteenth-century English life and religion. He was born in Exeter on 16 December 1714. This was the same day that Whitefield was born, and the same year as Howell Harris, William Romaine, and James Hervey, who all became prominent leaders in the Revival. From the age of eight until he was eighteen he attended Exeter Grammar School, and then, in 1732, entered Exeter College, Oxford. Contrary to the experience of some at this time, Walker did not fall into any laxity of life or morals but sought to study hard and live a moral and upright life. The eighteenth century is sometimes represented in an oversimplified way as a time of darkness and debauchery; actually the aim of many was to live in the way it was perceived that God desired. The aim of the Revival was to engage with all those who failed in this quest, whether or not they had fallen into a dissolute lifestyle. Wesley was a Fellow of Lincoln College at this time – situated a mere fifty yards from Exeter College – and the Holy Club was in full swing, though there is no evidence that Samuel Walker had any connection or involvement in Wesley's Oxford quests. Walker offered himself for ordination, as was so often the case, at the age of twenty-three, and was appointed in 1737 to be curate of Dodescomb Leigh, near Exeter. He remained there a year before travelling the continent for two years as a private tutor. He returned to become curate of Lanlivery, near Lostwithiel, and in 1740 became vicar of the parish in succession to Nicholas Kendall, who was also Archdeacon of Totnes, and who died in March 1740. However, in reality Walker was only keeping the living warm for the patron's nephew. He was diligent, caring, and conscientious. When the nephew came of age in 1746, Walker resigned and was appointed to the stipendiary curacy of Truro, where he laboured until his death in 1761.

In a 1756 letter, Walker recalled his ordination:

I remember the week before my ordination I spent with the other candidates – as dissolute, I fear as myself – in a very light and unbecoming manner; dining, supping, drinking and laughing together, when God knows, we should all have been on our knees, and warning each other to fear for our souls in the view of what we were about to put our hands to.[26]

As is often the case, this retrospective view carries the advantage of hindsight; the experience, however, was a common one. Individuals drifted into ordination in varying degrees of both personal and spiritual unpreparedness. Two years earlier, in 1754, he had described how unprepared he was for his post at Truro, "how utterly disqualified my heart and head were for my ministerial trust".[27] So, in July 1746, at thirty-one, Walker succeeded to the curacy at Truro. The town was well known for its pleasures and festivities. Clearly, Walker had knowledge of Christian doctrine, but "what he knew notionally, he neither felt nor sought practically".[28] The Revival was about both *felt* and *practical* religion, not instead of but alongside the classic doctrines. Walker's conversion came about through his friendship with George Conon, head of the grammar school in Truro and an evangelical convert. They first came into contact when Conon sought Walker's help in paying the duty on some imported wine – Conon, as a Christian, was uneasy at any thought of evading the required tax. Ryle, in his survey, skips over this experience rather lightly. What appears to have happened is that Walker got involved in conversations about salvation with Conon, the main consequence of which was that he realized that the nature of faith and assurance was not what he was experiencing in his own life. He later said that Conon was the first person he had met who was truly acquainted with Christ. He subsequently noted that "the change wrought upon me was slow, till under a variety of means I was brought to the knowledge of the truth as it is in Christ Jesus".[29]

This was clearly an evangelical conversion, though Walker, like Wesley and others, also experienced continued struggle. He suffered in particular from the desire to be held in high esteem by others – not something that Grimshaw battled with! He began to preach the necessity of repentance and the new birth. One feature of the Revival was that the preaching of the new birth provoked opposition. So it was for Walker, from both within and without his congregation. An early biographer refers to those who forsook the church on Sundays, fearing even his presence: "Let us go, here comes Walker."[30] The provenance of the remark is unclear, but it is reminiscent of certain features of Grimshaw's ministry. Certainly from 1748 onwards Walker's ministry had a noticeable impact, not least in the conversion of others and increasing numbers attending upon the preaching.

Walker's ministry

Walker placed great emphasis on the private spiritual guidance of the increasing numbers of individuals who approached him – by 1754 the number seeking such help exceeded 800.[31] There was also a remarkable change in the general life of what was in reality quite a small town, not least in the declining fortunes of the theatre and the cockfighting pit. Walker also set an example of holiness and integrity by, for example, resigning his additional post of Vicar of Talland because he now had scruples about non-residency (being vicar of a second parish but living elsewhere), despite the fact that it secured part of his income. He developed detailed schemes of private instruction for enquirers, including asking searching questions. He also had a particular impact on a regiment of soldiers stationed in Truro in 1756. He preached to them and more than a hundred came to him for private instruction, rising over time to 250. His efforts did not go unopposed. The captain of the regiment publicly forbade his soldiers to engage with Walker for spiritual sustenance. The regiment stayed in Truro for over two months; the officers ultimately expressed deep gratitude to Walker for his work. On the evening before their departure the soldiers gathered to hear Walker's exhortation. Ryle states that they "began their morning march praising God for having brought them under the sound of the gospel".[32] Whether that is an accurate description or not, the result was clearly significant. Letters from the soldiers themselves testified to the spiritual reality of Walker's work.

Another important feature of Walker's ministry was his development of the "clerical club", the Parsons' Club, for the evangelically minded clergy of the area. Membership was restricted to the clergy of the Church of England and those who accepted the Church's discipline and liturgy. Walker was not solely responsible, but he was the instigator and driving force. The membership hovered around six (rising to eleven), meeting monthly for support and encouragement.

Walker was utterly committed to the principles of the Established Church. William Grimshaw had scruples about preaching in other parishes but felt constrained to do so for the sake of the gospel. Walker rejected and resisted itinerancy from the beginning, restricting himself to his own parish and his clerical club, and remaining not only aloof from but also resistant to Methodist influences. This added to the complexity. Walker faced both opposition from clergy and bishops of the Established Church on charges of encouraging Methodism and resistance from those influenced by Methodism for standing apart from Wesley and his societies.

Opposition encountered

The propriety of making use of lay preachers exercised the evangelical clergy of the Established Church. Grimshaw had quickly embraced the principle of lay ministry, though he resisted lay ministers presiding over the sacrament of the Lord's Supper. Walker canvassed Wesley to exercise restraint in the matter of the lay preachers. The Wesleys sought to ensure high standards and to commit to never leaving the Church of England, and held that lay preachers should, if suitable, and in due time, be ordained. Walker directly reminded Wesley that the latter held ministerial office in the Church of England and expressed concern that the development of lay preachers would lead to separation. He viewed a possible split not only as undesirable but actually as unlawful, and also urged Wesley not to procrastinate but to ensure that the lay preachers were ordained or viewed as inspectors or readers in their societies rather than preachers. Lay preaching should be laid aside. Walker's views gained a stronger hearing with Charles than with John Wesley, the latter being unwilling to surrender the principle of the lay preacher.

This rather soured the relationship with John Wesley. Methodism was significant in Cornwall both inside and outside the Church of England. Some clergy openly welcomed the Methodist movement but there were also wider doctrinal differences. The position of most clergy who were sympathetic to the Methodists but remained firmly within the Church of England was the moderate Calvinism of Grimshaw, Venn, and Romaine. This stance enabled them to embrace the new-birth preaching of Wesley but resisted his overemphasis on free will and the possibility of Christian perfectionism.

John Wesley, however, was a crucial figure in the history of revival in Cornwall. He avoided preaching in Truro in deference to Walker and his ministry, but did not hold back from forming Methodist societies within the parishes of at least some of the evangelical clergy – a point of particular tension. The Wesleys were regular visitors to the region from 1743. Charles Wesley noted that the preachers were in demand five or six times daily and societies were springing up across the county. By 1746 there were four societies at Gwennap. Perhaps something of the tension between Walker and Wesley stemmed from the latter's already well-established foundations in the county before Walker experienced his change of heart.

Many of the early pioneers sought to co-operate with the Methodist revival because they not only saw the hand of God at work but they too had come under evangelical conviction. Grimshaw went further than Walker, but many Established Church ministers maintained an attachment to the Church of England, which can really only be explained in terms of the reformed doctrine adopted at the Reformation and the unique claims of the parochial system. Wesley urged his society members to continue to attend the parish church, but, as we noted earlier, in 1744 he called what would later be seen as the first Methodist Conference. Methodism was organizing, being nothing if not methodical.

CHAPTER 6

The Countess and her circle

The complex diversity of the Revival was played out in the middle of the eighteenth century through the ministries of some key figures whom we will look at in the next chapter. The glue that held the Revival together in these years was a female aristocrat, Selina, Countess of Huntingdon (1707–91). Her relationships were significant and obtained a hearing for the Revival where it might not otherwise have gained entry. She maintained sympathy and connections across the range of personalities involved, including the Moravians, but most importantly with George Whitefield. She established Methodism through chaplains and chapels. She brought the new birth into the drawing rooms of the aristocracy, where it was not always welcomed. Ultimately she gave form and shape to Calvinistic Methodism.

Upbringing and conversion

Selina was born on 24 August 1707 to Washington Shirley, the second Earl Ferrers, and his wife Mary. Theirs was a complicated family, divided by personal rivalry. She became the Countess of Huntingdon on her marriage in 1728 to Theophilus Hastings, the ninth Earl. We know little of Selina's religious upbringing but the family she married into certainly took religion seriously. The Earl's sisters, Margaret, Frances, and Anne, and his half-sister, Lady Betty, were all devout. Lady Betty supported Whitefield at Oxford, but her scruples for the order of the Church of England turned her against the Revival when Whitefield preached in the open air. She died in 1739. Lord and Lady Huntingdon had a happy marriage and Selina took her roles as wife and mother seriously. The couple lamented when they were apart from each other. Together they had seven children, only one of whom outlived the Countess. The Earl died in 1746. Selina's early married life was typical of that of any aristocrat. There was a degree of political intrigue, society gossip, concern with estates and property, and, of course, the social life of fashionable society. They were Tories and there was some suspicion of a degree of Jacobite sympathy (that is, for the claims of the Stuart dynasty). She was compassionate, took philanthropy seriously, baulked at the excess that sometimes characterized polite society, and certainly undertook her religious duties, but no more so than anyone else in her position.

The key period for Lady Huntingdon's conversion was June/July 1739. Lady Margaret had already adopted evangelical devotion, probably under the influence of Benjamin Ingham, who had preached in Lady Betty's private chapel. In 1738 the Bishop of Gloucester, the Earl's former tutor, wrote to him indicating his intention to ordain Whitefield – an almost apologetic letter craving her Ladyship's indulgence because she disapproved of Whitefield. Selina was not yet a Methodist. Lady Margaret, however, expressed her joy in her new-found faith in letters to Selina, and the Countess certainly seems to have responded with a positive desire to come to a true faith.

The Earl and Countess visited the Hastings family home of Ledston Hall in Yorkshire in the late spring or early summer of 1739, and so had direct contact with Lady Margaret for the first time since her conversion. We do not know the details of what followed beyond Lady Margaret's witness, Selina's searching, and the fact that Selina fell ill back home in her own residence of Donington Hall. Fear of mortality was ever present in this age and evangelicals were not afraid of using such things to bring individuals an eternal challenge. Thomas Haweis referred to Selina lifting her heart to Jesus and all distress and fears being removed. However, that description almost certainly reads back the piety into the moment of conversion. We do know that in 1766 the Countess, in a letter to Charles Wesley, referred to the prayer she had offered twenty-seven years earlier – which clearly places the occasion in 1739. Selina wrote at once to Lady Margaret on 26 July 1739, who replied that "my heart was so raised with gratitude to the ever blessed Jesus for the good work he had wrought in your Ladyship".[1] The joy was shared by two of Lady Margaret's sisters (Anne and Frances had both embraced the faith of the Revival), who snatched the letter from her hands. Selina, said Lady Margaret, in what would prove to be an understatement, "promises great things".[2] To Lady Betty, terminally ill, Selina wrote on 29 July 1739 that she considered there was nothing in the world that was equal to such piety. The Countess was converted. The degree to which the Earl shared her convictions is not clear. Certainly Selina wrote of his study of the Scriptures and he unquestionably tolerated his wife's new-found faith. The conversion was not so welcomed by all, including Selina's younger sister, Mary. Her letter speaks for itself.

> My compliments to Lady Margaret... but am sorry to find she is turned Methodist as this sect is so generally exploded that it's become a joke of all companies, and indeed I can go nowhere but I hear of the uncommon piety of the Donington family. I find it the general talk of every place. I'm concerned to think that my dear sister who is so reasonable in everything else should encourage such a canting set of people who place all their religion for the external show of it and pass uncharitable censures on them who are not in the same way of thinking.[3]

This quotation reveals a great deal about how others viewed the early adopters of evangelical piety. In fact, Lady Huntingdon was to do a great deal more than simply encourage these "canting... people". Lady Betty was also not impressed, and persuaded her confidant, Thomas Barnard, the master of Leeds Grammar School, to write to Selina, which he did, urging moderation and her silence! He suggested that her Ladyship should observe "moderation in all things", and that she "would admit but very few to any knowledge... of the business you have in hand".[4] Lady Margaret sent Benjamin Ingham to see Selina, which brought her under Moravian influence. She contributed to Moravian missionary causes but, as we have seen, there was a great deal of fluidity in the early relationships of the Revival, and Lady Huntingdon did not remain sympathetic to the Moravians for long. In November

1741 Lady Margaret and Benjamin Ingham married. This did nothing to encourage Lady Huntingdon's view of the Moravians. She was a child of her times, and shared the Earl's view of the match as one of social inequality.

Selina, Whitefield, and Wesley

By 1741 the Countess was in touch with the Wesleys, and at first the relationship was warm and friendly. John was a regular visitor to Selina's London home. The Countess was linked to the Fetter Lane Society and made contact with him within a few months of her conversion. In June 1741 they dined together and, probably by arrangement with Lady Huntingdon, Wesley headed to Leicestershire and Northamptonshire to organize the religious societies. This just happened to be the location of the Huntingdon family seat. Correspondence followed and on Sunday 28 June 1741 we know from Wesley's *Journal* that, although weary from the day's activities, he still rode to Lady Huntingdon's home, staying until 2 a.m. On 25 July Wesley preached the University Sermon at Oxford. It is widely thought that he abandoned his original text, "How is the faithful city become an harlot", under the influence of Selina during their discussions at the end of June. He was certainly with the Countess again at her Enfield home a few days after the sermon on 4 August, perhaps reporting back.

On the issue of "stillness", which divided the Wesleys from the Moravians, Selina sided firmly with John and Charles (and was active in ensuring Charles did not wobble!). She wrote to John Wesley on 24 October 1741 noting attacks from the "still ones", but also expressed her concern for Charles's firmness on the matter. When the Countess unexpectedly met George Whitefield in 1742, she not only rejected predestination but also advocated Wesleyan perfectionism. She complained that Whitefield "held forth above two hours upon the doctrine of election and reprobation", and that "no consideration that I was yet able to see from anything he had said could have any weight". What is more, in response to Whitefield's question on whether she lived without sin, she demurred but said "that there was such a state... [and]... that before we died it was absolutely necessary we should be in it".[5] The Lady was a Wesleyan.

In April she was still heaping praise on the Wesley brothers. However, she began to form a closer relationship with Charles, and it was at his suggestion that in 1743 she had a seat permanently reserved for her at Wesley's London chapel. John was less than impressed. This same year she was introduced to Howell Harris for the first time. In 1744 the Earl and Countess entertained those who attended the first Methodist Conference. Selina also established a friendship with the leading dissenting minister, Philip Doddridge, and under some influence from Harris began to attend Whitefield's Moorfields Tabernacle, especially in the run-up to his departure for the colonies in 1744. She began to invite her aristocratic friends to accompany her to listen to Whitefield. She was already at work among "the fine ladies of Bath".[6] Her doctrinal position was slowly shifting. By March 1744 she was in further contact with Harris and Whitefield; the former was clear that she was "right with God", "delivered from her own will", and "fitted for that great work".[7] Whitefield showed his own appreciation in a letter to Harris in 1746:

The good Countess has been there, and has been much pleased, I am told. She shines brighter and brighter every day… My poor prayers will be daily offered up to the God of all grace to keep her steadfast in the faith and to make her a burning and a shining light.[8]

Lord Huntingdon died at the age of forty-nine on 13 October 1746. In 1748 Whitefield returned from the colonies now assured that Lady Huntingdon was keen to work with him. Selina, however, had domestic and family matters to attend to, and this restricted her freedom in the 1750s.

The chaplains

On Whitefield's return Selina immediately appointed him as one of her chaplains. He was invited to preach to her aristocratic friends, and this aligned her closely with Whitefield and his Calvinism. Whitefield commented that he went "with fear and trembling, knowing how difficult it is to speak to the great so as to win them to Jesus Christ".[9] On 30 August 1748 Selina wrote excitedly to Philip Doddridge:

I must just tell you that I have had two large assemblies at my house of the mighty, the noble, the wise & the rich to hear the Gospel by Mr Whitefield and I have great pleasure in telling you they all expressed a great deal in hearing of him. Sometimes I do hope for Lord Chesterfield.[10]

The Lords Chesterfield and Bolingbroke were regular members of Lady Huntingdon's circle. They were, on one level, impressed. Bolingbroke described Whitefield as an extraordinary man of commanding eloquence, and Chesterfield said Whitefield's oratory was unrivalled and showed inexhaustible zeal. Its impact, however, was limited.[11] Nevertheless, the claim that the results of Lady Huntingdon's endeavours fell short of expectations, with the expected conversions failing to materialize, underestimates her influence.[12] There were some who came to associate closely with the Revival, including the Earl of Bath, who was a regular attendee at Whitefield's Tottenham Court Road chapel, established in 1756. Many others came under the influence of the gospel through Selina's strategic oversight. One of her circle, Lady Rockingham, prevailed on her to invite the Countess of Suffolk to hear Whitefield. She is reported to have sat out the sermon in silence and then flown into a rage and denounced what she had heard.[13] But one cannot accuse Lady Huntingdon of not having influence; the reaction it provoked, of course, was mixed.

Relationships between the Revival's great protagonists were increasingly complex. There were attempts at reconciliation and even some public shows of unity, but behind the scenes Wesley resented Whitefield becoming the recipient of Lady Huntingdon's favour and Whitefield fell out with Howell Harris. To be a chaplain to a member of the British aristocracy was not unusual, or especially important in itself. However, in this case a prominent proponent of the new birth became associated with a member of the peerage with significant influence and contacts. This combination was powerful, and was also the precursor to more formal organization within the Calvinist part of the Revival. Mark Noll points out that not only did Lady Huntingdon devote most of her wealth to the evangelical cause, but in addition "she was a critical factor in bringing an evangelical witness to the English aristocracy".[14]

Lady Huntingdon remained something of an enigma. She continued to pursue a good relationship with Wesley, who was respectful and responsive but less than keen. Whitefield was loyal, yet also continued to itinerate as well as visit the colonies. Howell Harris retreated to Wales. Perhaps surprisingly, the one who now gained a marked degree of favour with the Countess was Charles Wesley. Charles even felt able to express to her his resentment over being dominated by his brother.[15]

In the 1750s the Countess also supported Whitefield's fundraising efforts, first for his Moorfields Tabernacle and then for his chapel in Tottenham Court Road. As we shall see, the establishment of chapels began to raise some questions. Lady Huntingdon continued to develop her friendships with leading evangelical clergy and her ministry to the aristocracy. Key individuals who came into her wider circle at this time included James Hervey, William Romaine, Henry Venn, John Berridge, and John Fletcher. She was also willing to intervene, albeit not always successfully, in support of evangelical causes or individuals. In the early 1750s she tried to help Moses Browne, who was denied ordination. Her Ladyship wrote to various bishops, to no avail, and then through her range of contacts obtained the result she desired. Browne was appointed to Olney, the living which was later given to John Newton. Lady Huntingdon, along with Whitefield, was also involved in continued clashes with the Moravians. It is ironic that the group that was so foundational for the development of the uniquely evangelical take on experience became the focus of such discord. Under von Zinzendorf the Moravians became very focused on "the wounds of Jesus" and his physical sufferings, as well as on the issue of stillness. Wesley too, as we have noted, departed from their company.

The chapels

Whitefield concluded that Bristol needed a tabernacle like the one at Moorfields. Lady Huntingdon had a home in Clifton, in the Bristol suburbs, and had close ties to a society linked to Whitefield, which boasted many aristocratic members. She actively solicited funds to support the project. Both the new Moorfields and the Bristol tabernacles were opened in 1753. In March 1754 Whitefield departed for the American colonies on his fifth expedition, which lasted until May 1755. His regular absences had a significant and negative impact on the development and leadership of the Calvinist branch of the Revival. In 1758 Selina's youngest son, Henry, died, leaving just her daughter, also Selina, in the family home. Sadly, she too died just five years later. In 1759, with fear of a French invasion rife, Selina gathered the evangelical leaders to pray, including both Wesley and Whitefield – they were all good old Tories. Ironically, the distress that befell her family freed her for new efforts in the 1760s, though one biographer claims that by this time "the opportunities for her to use her influence outside the movement, or to offer wise counsel within it, were narrowing".[16] However, the Countess was not finished yet.

In 1761 Selina opened a chapel in the fashionable south-coast town of Brighton, adjacent to a house she had acquired. Whitefield had preached in Brighton, the resort was expanding, and Selina had been there in the late 1750s so that Henry could convalesce. The opening of chapels at Moorfields, Bristol, and now Brighton raised the important question of their relationship to the wider Church of England. She appointed numerous chaplains from the ranks of the evangelical clergy of the Established Church. However, unlike in the Methodist meeting houses for the religious societies, the presence of these chaplains in Lady Huntingdon's chapels meant there would be regular services and celebrations of the Lord's Supper that were open to the public – an alternative to the parish church.

The key dilemma that Lady Huntingdon faced was whether to register the chapels as dissenting meeting houses under the Toleration Act of 1689. If the evangelicals were to obtain their desired freedom to operate, they needed to effectively declare themselves dissenters. Otherwise, they had no right to build or provide worship services outside the provisions of the Established Church. One should not underestimate the strength of the attachment of the majority of evangelical leaders, especially in the Calvinist branch of the Revival, to the Established Church of England. However, there was an ingenious solution. There was a long-standing and generally accepted practice within the Church of England of members of the aristocracy providing private chapels. These were attached to their homes and outside the jurisdiction of the bishop. A chaplain could be appointed and, perhaps most interesting of all, members of the public could be invited to attend. All the early chapels established by the Countess of Huntingdon were attached to homes that she owned or leased. Naturally, she was not always present, and indeed the houses were sometimes let to tenants. At Ote Hall in Wivelsfield the Countess rented the house and converted part into a chapel

– at some point after its opening William Romaine reported a hundred communicants.

In 1764–65 Selina moved to construct a chapel in Bath. Its architecture was remarkable, its ecclesiastical management rather complex. She now had to staff three chapels and deal with evangelical clergy who had differing views on the propriety of preaching outside their own parish, as well as the need to discharge their own responsibilities. Lady Huntingdon, with perhaps surprising support from Lord Chesterfield, opened a chapel at his country mansion, Bretby Hall in Derbyshire. Others were opened in Lewes, Tunbridge Wells, and elsewhere. Howell Harris, after a long period of illness and withdrawal from the revival scene, was now back at work, having established a Christian community at Trevecca. He supplied the chapels' pulpits, alongside her regular chaplains.

The college

When William Romaine (see Chapter 7) became the first evangelical to obtain a living in London, at St Ann's, Blackfriars (finally secured in 1766 after court action), one consequence was that he was far less available to the Countess. At the same time Thomas Haweis and Martin Madan became involved in an unseemly dispute with the patron of a living over an advowson (the property right to the appointment to a benefice), which distracted their attention. Lady Huntingdon needed to make longer-term provision for the supply of her pulpits. Working with Howell Harris she sought to implement a vision, long shared by him, for an academy or school for preachers. They secured a building close to Trevecca and work began to enlarge and equip it towards the end of 1767. In classic evangelical fashion, this college would both provide for intellectual equipping, as an alternative to the universities (six students had recently been expelled from Oxford for holding Calvinist beliefs), and be a place for practical preparation for an itinerant preaching ministry. Illustrating the complexity of relationships within the Revival, Lady Huntingdon secured the services of the anti-Calvinist Methodist – and Vicar of Madeley in Shropshire – the Reverend John Fletcher, as the first principal of the college. Fletcher described Selina as a soul devoted to Jesus. With the stated aim of equipping prospective students for ministry in the Church of England, the college opened in August 1768. Fletcher was the president, while remaining Vicar of Madeley. Tutors and students were recruited, including two of those expelled from Oxford, and, through the ministry of Fletcher, a collier named James Glazebrook. Fletcher drew up a curriculum. The opening ceremony was on 24 August 1768, Selina's sixty-first birthday, and George Whitefield presided over the proceedings, just two weeks after the death of his wife. Among other things students were required to give weight to "practical divinity", which involved regular preaching tours. The college's future was not to be straightforward, but its establishment solved the immediate problem of pulpit supply. Visitors in the weeks that followed the opening ceremony included Charles Wesley. In running the college, however, John Fletcher was less than impressed with the students' spiritual state.

Spa Fields, ordinations, and the establishment of the Connexion

To complete the story of Selina we need to leap ahead a little. George Whitefield died in Massachusetts on 30 September 1770. Selina had last seen him with Charles Wesley at her home in February 1769. At Trevecca there were problems over the supply of books and clothing, diet, and the college's spiritual underpinning. William Williams, another prominent figure in the Welsh Revival, complained that some students arrived without a clear calling, and others were sent there by their parents with no intent to finance them! John Wesley turned up for the first anniversary, marked by preaching in both English and Welsh. For the second anniversary in 1770 the Countess of Huntingdon made it clear to Wesley that he was not welcome. She was reacting against the minutes of Wesley's Methodist Conference of that year, which she interpreted as suggesting that a person could contribute to their own salvation – a reassertion of the classic disputes over Calvinism and free will that marred the Revival. Selina took up Whitefield's mantle. Wesley wrote her a letter that has not survived, but which stirred up rather than calmed the waters. Selina dismissed a Trevecca master, Joseph Benson, for lack of clarity on the matter in 1771 and demanded that the students write a piece rejecting the minutes. In March 1771 John Fletcher gave Lady Huntingdon his own justification for what the minutes contained, and resigned. The row, exaggerated by each side's misinterpretation of the other, exploded into the public arena. Fletcher argued that Calvinism risked falling into antinomianism (that is, licence). Wesley was denounced as a papist and the vitriolic pamphlet war continued. Lady Huntingdon did not support the level of polemic and she gradually renewed both friendship and contact with the Wesleys and with John Fletcher in the middle years of the 1770s.

Whitefield's death was a blow for the Countess. Wesley preached the memorial sermon at the Tottenham Court Road chapel; Selina did not attend, but instead invited Henry Venn to preach a sermon in Bath. Charles Wesley wrote a sympathetic letter to her. The major problem for the Calvinist wing was the extent to which it would contain itself within the boundaries of the Established Church. The Wesleys were clear that the Revival belonged within and not without. Two quite strange things happened. The Wesleyan Revival was better organized and, against the wishes of its founders, though not necessarily contrary to their actions, a formal division occurred that flourished as Methodism. The Calvinist wing, less well organized though with more influence among existing evangelical clergy, formally separated and did not flourish. The reason was that most of those of Calvinist conviction within the Church of England stayed. The Church of England was their church.

Selina too was a passionate adherent of the Established Church. She did not, however, have the same investment in it as the ordained Wesleys. Her hope was that Trevecca would supply candidates for ordination to the Church of England. The reality was that only a handful managed to achieve this, and students from the college were treated with much suspicion. Lady Huntingdon, in good old-fashioned evangelical style, was equally suspicious of the bench of bishops. Finding a curacy, the "title" post with all the necessary testimonials, was as problematic then as it sometimes is even today for evangelicals. The traditional dissenting congregations were often equally difficult.

In 1774 the Countess became interested in buying a building in the Clerkenwell area of London. But her move was not successful and a group of businessmen stepped in, purchased the building, and registered it as a dissenting chapel. Northampton Chapel opened in 1777 and two evangelical ministers of the Church of England, Herbert Jones and William Taylor, agreed to provide the services. The curate of St James, Clerkenwell, asserted his rights against the two clergy and laid charges in the Bishop of London's consistory court. Jones and Taylor were convicted of preaching in a dissenting chapel and conducting worship in a parish to which they were not licensed. They were silenced and the chapel closed. The Countess made her move and acquired the lease. Some 5,000 people were attending the chapel. She wrote to the Bishop of London to tell him that her purpose in taking the chapel under her protection was to prevent thousands from becoming dissenters.[17] Alterations were made to the chapel, which was closed for two weeks. The work included the provision of accommodation for the Countess – after all, this was yet another personal chapel of a peeress of the realm. In 1774 Selina had appointed Thomas Haweis, an evangelical of the Established Church, as one of her personal chaplains, and he presided over the opening on 28 March 1779 of Spa Fields Chapel. Within two weeks William Sellon, the curate of St James, Clerkenwell, instituted proceedings in the consistory court. He insisted that Haweis required his permission to preach in the chapel. Haweis claimed the privileged protection of the rights of the peerage to provide chapels and that the matter was outside the court's jurisdiction. The court adjourned for five months. In November it reconvened, this time with a further claim lodged against Cradock Glascott, a second chaplain, denying his right to preach at Spa Fields. The prosecution case was simple: a chapel with seating for thousands, a public entrance, and tickets sold for seating, could not in any sense be construed as private. The edifice Selina had built on a rather shaky foundation was about to fall.

In May 1780 judgment was given against Haweis. The case against Glascott, and, of course, in time her other preachers, was now entirely predictable. The only avenue open to the Countess to protect her chapels was to register them under the Toleration Act as dissenting meeting houses. Glascott removed himself to Devon, but a third chaplain, Thomas Wills, decided to secede. Lady Huntingdon had already realized there was little hope. She told her clergy supporters that she was ready to go to prison with them, and in a letter to a former student declared, "I am to be cast out of the Church for what I have been doing these forty years – speaking and living for Jesus Christ."[18] In his statement Wills explained his grounds for secession – as so often the case with evangelical secessions from the Established Church, the baptismal office (and the presumption of regeneration) and the burial service (with the equally bold claim to eternal life). William Taylor, one of the original ministers, joined the secession, but Haweis and Glascott did not. On 9 March 1783, Wills and Taylor presided over what were, in effect, the Connexion's first ordinations, of six students. Others followed. None of the well-known names – Romaine, Venn, Berridge or Walter Shirley – supported the Countess. Some evangelical clergy of the Established Church still preached in her chapels, and indeed many did not immediately register as dissenting chapels, but the die was cast.

Selina was seventy-five years old at the time of the first ordinations, and her health was not especially robust. The Connexion was now established but was quite simply too dependent on her. The pressure of organization and finance was significant. As her chapels became more established they tended to prefer a settled pastoral ministry to itinerancy. Nevertheless, there was some expansion, with five new chapels in the first five months of 1785 alone. A further question concerned the future of the college at Trevecca, which had long depended on her financial support. In these closing years further tensions could not be avoided, including a theological split over the nature of Calvinism among the ministers of Spa Fields Chapel. Wills was dismissed but the other ministers also followed in later years; the Connexion relied too greatly on an elderly peeress. When Lady Huntingdon died, on 17 June 1791, control of the Connexion passed to the beneficiaries of her will, who ironically included Thomas Haweis, who had remained with the Church of England. Lady Anne Erskine, who had long assisted Selina, took on the running of the Connexion. Trevecca closed but a new college opened at Cheshunt.

Lady Huntingdon's importance cannot be overstated. She exemplified both the strengths and the weaknesses of the Revival. Tenacity, commitment, passion, a love that extended across the theological divisions, and a desire to remain within the bounds of the Church of England were all hallmarks of a significant section of the Evangelical Revival. Some poor judgments, a lack of proper planning and provision, and even a lack of focus all contributed to the rather modest success of her enterprise. However, the gospel prospered through her and perhaps the last word should go to the evangelical minister of the Established Church, John Berridge, who, on her death, remarked, "Another pillar is gone to glory. Mr Whitefield is gone, Mr Wesley and his brother are gone, and I shall go soon."[19]

CHAPTER 7

The consolidation of the Revival

The early pioneers of the 1740s and 1750s were dynamic, innovative individuals who took Revival doctrines to heart and sought to bring the challenge of the new birth to their parishes and beyond. As we have seen, while the Wesleys (but mainly John) and Whitefield itinerated regularly, others undertook regional circuits or tours, while some remained strictly within the parish boundaries. In the middle of the century this pattern was extended through the ministries of a wider group of clergy. There are many characters to choose from, but in reviewing the Revival's progress in the 1760s and 1770s four particular figures emerge: Henry Venn (1724–97), William Romaine (1714–95), John Newton (1725–1807), and John Fletcher (1729–85). Through them we see all the challenges and themes of the Revival emerge alongside the story itself. In the background, as ever, remains George Whitefield (until his death in 1770) and, of course, the brothers Wesley – not forgetting the Countess.

Background and conversion

The background of the four was as varied as the locations of their births. William Romaine, of French Huguenot extraction, was born in Hartlepool in 1714. His father was a merchant. Henry Venn was born on 2 March 1724 in Barnes, south-west London, into a clergy family. Venn and Romaine were educated at local schools. Romaine entered Hertford College, Oxford, in 1730 (or 1731) and subsequently moved to Christ Church, obtaining an MA degree in 1737, a year after his ordination as deacon by the Bishop of Hereford. In 1738 he was ordained to the priesthood and nominated curate of Banstead. In June 1742, Venn went to the other place and entered St John's College, Cambridge, and then moved to Jesus College owing to the availability of a scholarship. (Some things don't change!) He took his BA in 1745, was ordained in 1747, and was then elected to a Fellowship of Queens' College, gaining his MA and remaining at Queens' until his marriage in 1757. Venn and Romaine, brought up in a clerical and a mercantile family respectively, both reflected the polite godliness of pre-Revival England. Venn was moral and upright, influenced by Law's "Serious Call". He fasted and prayed. He served a number of curacies, distributed tracts to the poor, and provoked the ire of some fellow clergy as a result. He was described as a Methodist, but a Methodist he was not.

As for John Newton, many aspects of his life are of interest to students of the Revival. The landmarks of his early life include the impact of the death of his mother in 1732, when Newton was just seven years old. By the age of eleven he was at sea with his father's merchant ships. Slowly but surely he was stepping away from the spiritual influences of the dissenting congregation that his mother had attended. In 1744 Newton was press-ganged into His Majesty's navy. The intervention of his father saw him promoted to midshipman. The following year, the attractions of his future wife, Polly, led him to desert. Arrested and returned to the ship, he was flogged and demoted. He was subsequently exchanged for a merchant seaman – a common practice at the time. This led to his introduction to Africa and the slave trade.

Jean Guillaume de la Fléchère – known to us as John Fletcher – was a remarkable individual, a committed Arminian, close associate of the Wesleys, first principal of the Calvinist Countess's Trevecca College, and the Vicar of Madeley in Shropshire for twenty-five years. Fletcher was born in Switzerland on 12 September 1729. He left an account of his early years, though this suffers from the usual problem of overstating both religious experience and depth of temptation. Writing to Charles Wesley in 1757, Fletcher recalled, "I was about 7 years old when the Lord made thus his goodness to pass before me for the first time," and "When I was About ten years of age, I began to give up all and to sell myself under sin being surrounded on every side by temptations & drawn in by bad examples."[1] The date of the letter, after Fletcher's conversion, illustrates the problem. Clearly it was impossible to grow up in Switzerland without coming under both the cultural and the theological influence of Calvinism. He matriculated in the University of Geneva in 1746, aged seventeen. His parents thought he was destined for church ministry, but, perhaps not surprisingly in the more liberal environment of eighteenth-century Geneva, he did not share this view, and became a soldier. Information on his military service is rather sketchy, and it was only three years or so after entering the university that he arrived in London.

Each of these characters experienced evangelical conversion. For Newton it happened in 1748, and around the same time for Romaine. For Venn it was a gradual process in the years up to 1754, also the year (or possibly 1755) of Fletcher's conversion. Newton's story is as exciting as any adventure novel. His experience in Africa was an unpleasant combination of conflict, exploitation, and breakdowns in professional relationships. In 1747 he managed to extricate himself with a passage home on the trading ship *Greyhound*. Newton fell out with the captain. In March 1748 the ship was rocked by a violent storm. It appeared that the ship would be lost and Newton uttered his famous words seeking the Lord's mercy, to the shock of his crewmates. By April the ship reached Ireland, with Newton a converted and changed man. His story, though, was only just beginning. Invited that year to take command of a slave trader, the *Brownlow,* Newton actually accepted the post of mate – second in command. He went through spiritual turmoil on the voyage, which included months of slave operations in Africa. He returned to Liverpool in 1749 and the following year married his beloved Polly. There followed fifteen months in charge of another slave trader, the *Duke of Argyle.* Circumstances were grim. A further command followed, that of the *African,* but there is also evidence of a deepening spiritual and prayer life. In 1754 Newton appeared to be having doubts about the slave trade when he was struck down by illness; although only twenty-nine years old, he had to resign his captaincy, and his seafaring career was over. In 1755 he met Whitefield, became tide surveyor of Liverpool, and welcomed George to speak there, followed two years later by Wesley.

Venn's more gradual experience occurred independently of the wider Revival. He drew a distinction in Law's writings between two rival claims: the primacy of excellent moral character and the blood of Christ. This led him to reject Law and turn directly to the Scriptures. He realized that he could not impose on others a standard (moral excellence) that he could not attain himself. Consequently he came to the classic evangelical position of reliance on the work of Christ as the sole and all-sufficient ground of salvation. His association with the players and doctrines of the wider Revival lay ahead of him. He became curate of Clapham in 1754 (and hence was non-resident in his Fellowship) and three years later, in 1757, he married.

As for Fletcher, after his arrival in London he learned to speak English and became tutor to the sons of the Member of Parliament for Shrewsbury, Thomas Hill. This introduced Fletcher to Shropshire, which he described as beautiful and fertile.[2] As tutor his time was split between the family's London and country homes. As he journeyed between the two houses he encountered Methodist sympathizers and began to make contact with evangelical congregations in London. So it was that in 1754 or 1755 (depending on which scholar is believed) he underwent conversion. One of the Hills was also converted, although the activities of their increasingly zealous tutor did cause the family some embarrassment. Despite being foreign, Fletcher was ordained in 1757 as curate of Madeley in rural Shropshire, a living under the control of the Hill family. In 1760 he succeeded to the living, a move supported by Charles Wesley and Lady Huntingdon but opposed by John

Wesley, who really wanted him in London to assist with the wider Methodist work.

Ministry

Two years after his marriage – that is, in 1759 – Henry Venn moved to Huddersfield, which his son described later as "the grand scene of his labours in the Church".[3] Yet even while at Clapham, Venn had been in correspondence with Wesley, attended his Conference in Oxford in 1756, itinerated with George Whitefield (who preached twice at Clapham), and stayed with the Countess of Huntingdon. He had crossed the line. He set out the reason for his move: "Grieved at the obstinate rejection of the Gospel during five years by almost all the rich (and there were but few poor in the place), I accepted a living unexpectedly offered to me by my very affectionate friend, the Earl of Dartmouth."[4] Once in Huddersfield, as they did with his neighbour William Grimshaw, the crowds flocked to his preaching, which they had not done in Clapham. Huddersfield was a significant living with a population numbered in thousands. Also like Grimshaw, he laboured to such an extent among his flock that his health suffered severely. The parish was a large one and Venn took very seriously the practice, often neglected, of visiting the numerous villages and teaching house meetings in each place. He preached up to ten times a day during the week as well as on Sundays. In Clapham he had experienced opposition rather than success; in Huddersfield it was opposition as well as success. He wrote to Thomas Atkinson in 1764, saying, "You will be pleased to hear that the work of the Lord prospers exceedingly in many souls."[5] The usual accusations of antinomianism were made (neglecting good works and hence encouraging laziness). In Huddersfield the next shift in his faith and ministry occurred with his adoption of more Calvinist views. The reasons for the change in focus are not entirely clear. John Venn claims that the key factors were his father's experience of suffering, and a greater appreciation of the corruption and frailty of human nature. Certainly suffering can lead to a greater appreciation of God's grace and less reliance on human strength. However, his wife, who reacted with some vigour against ideas of Christian perfectionism, may also have been influential. The change in view took place in the first few years after his acceptance of the living of Huddersfield.

In an age of neglect, Newton turned to parish ministry with diligence. He preached several times a week and conducted morning and evening prayer on Sundays. He often preached for an hour at each and apart from on Sunday was rarely seen in clerical attire. As well as preaching from the pulpit he also conducted a house-to-house ministry. He held mid-week meetings where hymns were introduced (like many, though not all, evangelical clergy in the Established Church, Newton was opposed to the introduction of hymns in the Sunday service). His ministry had a good effect (though a negative one on the local dissenting congregations), and numbers of both locals and visitors grew. Like many of the Revival leaders, Newton rose early (at 5 a.m.), spending two hours in prayer and Bible reading.

In 1767 Newton first met William Cowper. The relationship was creative and flourished despite its many challenges – a point emphasized by Cowper's depression. Together they wrote hymns, a characteristic feature of the Revival but one which was unusual in church life at the time. The Olney hymn book eventually emerged in 1779. Cowper suffered from hallucinations, nightmares, and suicidal thoughts. Newton cared for him throughout as a pastor. New Year's Day 1773 saw the first production of "Amazing Grace". Newton's circle of friends and confidants continued to expand. He preached in many other pulpits and churches but did not itinerate outside his own parish without permission. In 1779 he was approached to become the Rector of St Mary, Woolnoth, in the heart of the City of London. The stipend – six times greater than that of Olney – would certainly assist his personal finances. After Romaine, Newton was the second clergyman to hold a living in London – a prospect which provoked some opposition in the House of Lords. In his opening sermon, Newton made clear to the congregation his responsibility to set out evangelical truth before them: "The Bible is the grand repository of the truths that it will be the business and pleasure of my life to set before you."[6] Newton was the classic moderate Calvinist that typified Revival ministers within the Church of England. He described himself as more of a Calvinist than anything else, but, like a lump of sugar in a cup of tea, Calvinism was best offered mixed and diluted! Other evangelical clergy were emerging in London: Richard Cecil (St John's, Bedford Row), Henry Foster (St James, Clerkenwell), John Venn (Holy Trinity, Clapham); with Newton and others they formed the Eclectic Society. The famous Clapham Sect (a later and rather disparaging description, of course) was also coming into prominence. In 1785 Newton received a letter from William Wilberforce, seeking spiritual counsel in the light of his own conversion experience and uncertain whether his calling was to withdraw from public life or to embrace it. Wilberforce joined Newton's congregation as he gave public expression to his faith. Newton's advice to Wilberforce was to take up the mantle of Christianity in public life, and by October 1787 Wilberforce had resolved to campaign against the slave trade. The consequences of that are well known to history. Within a few months the powerful testimony of John Newton was in the public domain. Newton's ministry continued and he survived into the early years of the next century.

Fletcher told John Wesley that the parish of Madeley was a door providentially opened, and, "I cannot leave those many sheep in the wilderness, before I have exhausted myself in crying to them to turn in the name of the Lord."[7] This reveals how in a relatively short time Fletcher moved into the heart of the relationships that nourished the evangelical movement. He first met the Countess of Huntingdon in November 1759, before his institution to the living of Madeley, describing her as "a humble and pious Countess".[8] We also know that by 1760 he was in touch with John Berridge, Vicar of Everton, Bedfordshire, and a leading Revival personality. Fletcher feared the oppression of the bishop, or even that "the Bishop to whom I am, or shall be known for a Methodist may refuse to institute me".[9] He later complained about the Bishop of Lichfield's inactivity, and objections which were raised against his status (including not being a naturalized citizen). He was also under some threat having been caught preaching in one of Wesley's London chapels by the chaplain to the Bishop of Hereford![10] Fletcher was a key ally of Wesley, and his skills were greatly needed in the organization of the fledgling Methodist movement. His description of what he found in his parish is salutary:

Form, if you can, an idea of the misery of men,
kneeling, stooping, or lying on one side, to toil all
day in a confined space, where a child could hardly
stand; whilst a younger company, with their hands
and feet on the black dusty ground, and a chain about
their body, creep and drag along, like four-footed
beasts, heavy loads of the dirty mineral... Destructive
damps, and clouds of noxious dust, infect the air they
breathe. Sometimes water incessantly distils on their
naked bodies; or, bursting upon them in streams,
drowns them, and deluges their work. At other times,
pieces of detached rocks crush them to death, or the
earth breaking in upon them buries them alive. And
frequently sulphurous vapours, kindled in an instant by
the light of their candles, form subterraneous thunder
and lightning...[11]

Approximately eighty years later, another evangelical, the
Earl of Shaftesbury, forced an end to such practices for the
children involved. On his second Sunday, Fletcher preached
to eighty people. A year later he reported full aisles (though
we have no numbers) and conversions. He remarked that he
was having trouble with one woman's visions. He implored
Charles Wesley to encourage the Kingswood miners to pray
for the Madeley colliers. He noted that he faced opposition
in the parish. He wanted to preach in some of the outlying
villages within the parish and the formation of a religious
society now provided that opportunity. A year after his
arrival John Wesley was still trying to entice him away and
Fletcher was still pleading the case of divine providence in
keeping him in Madeley. In 1761 he complained to Charles

about a neighbouring cleric's anti-Methodist sermon at the archdeacon's visitation. Fletcher made clear that he had written to the clergyman concerned, "in which I touched upon the principal errors of his discourse as politely and firmly as I am able".[12] He was a strong supporter of the traditional evangelical contention of the scriptural foundations of the Established Church. He also shared the Revival ministers' standard anti-Catholicism. He began to itinerate from around 1764 in neighbouring parishes, usually in Wesley's meeting houses or Selina's chapels. In April 1765 he "sacrificed the last remnant of my reputation"[13] by preaching in the open air for the first time. Even his friends expected him to be turned out of his living. He described how this field preaching caused a storm, but the bishop had not yet intervened to try to prevent this ministry.

In the same year he founded a clerical association in Worcester in the West Midlands, bringing six evangelical clergymen together. Fletcher makes numerous references to his preaching among the colliers at Coalpit Bank – the Kingswood of Shropshire was how he described it – and he reported many conversions. From this time Fletcher suffered significant bouts of ill health, requiring three years in Switzerland (where the magistrate forbade him to preach out of doors); he finally returned to England in 1781. He promptly married, made a claim to Christian perfection (in line with Wesley, but which William Cowper thought conceited), and, despite John Wesley's continued attempts to get Fletcher to London, he and his wife rebuilt the Christian work in Madeley, which had suffered in his absence.

Conflicts

In 1748 Romaine was nominated for the vacant lectureship of St Botolph's, Billingsgate. Lectureships often had their origins with the Puritans and were sometimes endowed, and the nomination did not usually lie with the Rector. In some instances appointment was by congregational election. These were opportunities for evangelical clergy when they found it hard to obtain livings as rectors. This unusual provision also allowed for evangelicals to gain their first footholds in the capital. The following year, 1749, Romaine was elected to the afternoon lectureship of St Dunstan's in the West, in Fleet Street. There were in fact two lectureships at St Dunstan's, one endowed and the other supported by voluntary parish contributions. Romaine was preaching the doctrines of the Revival, and the Rector was ill-disposed towards these claims. He also itinerated on behalf of the Countess of Huntingdon. Romaine complained of the problems, remarking, "I have had sad troubles at St Dunstan's with the new vicar. He will let none preach for me without a licence, which puts me to great inconvenience: but all is governed by One, who knows what is best."[14] The Rector sought to prevent Romaine from occupying the pulpit at the agreed time of the lecture. In 1762 the matter reached the High Court. Romaine was deprived of the parish lectureship but confirmed in the endowed post, with the use of the church granted to him for the exercise of the lectureship – at 7 p.m. The wardens declined to open the church until the hour of the lecture or to light the building. Hence he often preached by candlelight. This led to crowds gathering in the street as they waited for admission to the church. The Bishop of London then intervened on Romaine's behalf and ordered the time of the service to be adjusted to 6 p.m. and for the church to be opened and lit in good time. Romaine also took the post of assisting the morning preacher at St George's, Hanover Square, in 1750. He relinquished this in 1755 after complaints that the crowds that flocked to hear him were preventing the pew holders from getting to their seats. In 1755 Romaine married, at the age of forty. He took an additional position at St Olave's, Southwark, until 1759. He preached before the University of Oxford on several occasions. After two sermons in 1757 under the title "the Lord our righteousness", the university pulpit was denied him. He wrote to the Vice-Chancellor to challenge him to publicly state where he had departed from the Scriptures or the doctrines of the Reformation. In 1763 he preached at Haworth, shortly after the death of his friend William Grimshaw.

Romaine became the first evangelical to be nominated to a living in the City of London when he was proposed as Rector of St Ann's, Blackfriars, and St Andrew-by-the-Wardrobe in 1764. As was so often the case with him, it was not plain sailing. The patronage of the living alternated between the Crown and the parishioners, and on the death of the previous incumbent, the presentation fell to the parishioners. Without Romaine's knowledge some put his name forward. The date set for the preaching "hustings" was 30 September 1764. Many of his regular hearers stayed away to ensure they did not crowd out or alienate the local parishioners (and voters). Romaine made it clear that he would not canvass for votes. At the close of the poll, a dispute broke out over eligibility to vote. A second poll was held and he emerged the winner. His opponents appealed to the courts. In February 1766 the Lord Chancellor declared in favour of Romaine and ordered him to be instituted. Romaine had his own reservations: "I am frightened to think of watching over two or three thousand when it is work enough to watch over one. The plague of my own heart almost wearies me to death; what can I do with so vast a number!"[15] There was clear support for Romaine within the parish. When he proposed to preach a series of sermons on the Church of England's Thirty-nine Articles a group of thirty parishioners, including the churchwardens, urged him to publish them, a request he did not comply with. Romaine sought to ensure the proper conduct of worship – he protested against the practice of not only arriving late but in some instances just turning up for the sermon. He also objected strongly to the practice of chatter, talking, and conversation in church after the service, always retiring to his house for such discussion. As with the other evangelical divines of the period, his commitment was unswerving. He took breakfast at six in the morning, held family prayers twice a day, and retired to bed at ten in the evening. He even insisted on preaching his normal Thursday evening lecture at St Dunstan's on the day he heard of the death of his second son in the East Indies, despite the protestations of his wife.

John Newton's story took a turn of some significance for the course and cause of the Revival after the end of his seafaring days. He resolved to seek ordination into the Church of England – a decision that led to another contest between the Established Church and its evangelical clergy and aspirants. In 1758 Newton visited Yorkshire, and met Henry Venn. He described "a flourishing county, like Eden in the garden of the Lord watered on every side by the streams of the gospel".[16] This was, in Newton's eyes, undoubtedly the consequence of the presence of divines such as Venn and Grimshaw. It was also excessive Romanticism. He wrestled with the call to ordination and indeed with which denomination to join. He had some doubts over baptism, the Prayer Book, the attitude towards evangelicals, and the freedom to preach the cross of Christ. However, he resolved that it was the Church of England in which he should serve. Armed with the offer of a curate's post (a title) from Henry Crooke of Leeds, he approached the Bishop of Chester, his local prelate. The bishop claimed that Crooke's parish was under the jurisdiction of the Archbishop of York, and declined to ordain Newton. The archbishop in turn hid behind obscure rules which stated that candidates for Holy Orders required a degree from Oxford or Cambridge, though these had long been disregarded.

In 1759 Newton sought to approach the Archbishop of York directly, but was rebuffed. He asked the Bishop of Chester again, and the answer was once again negative. Newton toyed with the idea of independence, but many urged him to be patient. The Countess of Huntingdon discussed Newton's plight with the Earl of Dartmouth, who was the patron of the living of Olney. He had offered the post to Thomas Haweis – an evangelical forced out of the living of St Mary Magdalene, Oxford. Haweis deferred to Newton. Armed with the offer of a living and the necessary testimonials, Newton was again ready to seek ordination. Dartmouth persuaded the Bishop of Chester to add his own name to the testimonials – despite having twice rejected Newton for ordination – and Newton then approached the Bishop of Lincoln, in whose diocese Olney lay. The bishop sent him to the new Archbishop of York (another passing of the buck), and on the day before the archbishop intended to hold an ordination, his secretary rebuffed Newton. With evangelical zeal and gritty determination, on 13 April 1764 Newton sought out

Dartmouth, who wrote a personal appeal to the archbishop. The archbishop declined to ordain but, acting outside his powers, assured Newton that the diocesan bishop would do so. Dartmouth intervened again, with a personal meeting with the Bishop of Lincoln. The bishop interviewed Newton who, in classic evangelical style, unhelpfully disclosed his doubts about the Prayer Book! Nevertheless, on 29 April 1764 Newton was finally ordained in the private chapel of the Bishop of Lincoln – "my only hope is in the name and power of Jesus".[17]

John Fletcher adopted many classic evangelical methods, including cottage meetings for the workers, which brought him close to prosecution under the Conventicle Act – part of the infamous Clarendon Code Acts of 1660–62 to suppress non-conformity. In a letter to Charles Wesley in 1762 he noted that a neighbouring clergyman "has openly declared war on me",[18] and the magistrate sought to enforce the Act's provision against gatherings for worship in private houses. Two of Fletcher's parishioners were arrested and he appeared before the magistrate on their behalf, with the neighbouring clergyman also present. The magistrate threatened to enforce the Act even if the meeting took place in Fletcher's own house. Fletcher stood firm: "I assured him that we were prepared to bear the severity of the law if it applied to us."[19] The magistrate then went to a higher court to seek a warrant for Fletcher's arrest, but the other justices denied the application on the grounds that the matter was one for ecclesiastical jurisdiction rather than for the secular courts. He then faced his churchwardens threatening to take him to the Ecclesiastical Courts for the same offence![20] Like so many of his friends in the Revival he faced ridicule and opposition from both parishioners and fellow clergy: "On my arrival I found everyone prejudiced against me, and above all the Clergy of the neighbourhood... There is not a single one whom I can consider a Servant of God."[21] In 1762 he told Charles Wesley that "the opposition people make to my ministry grows".[22]

Beliefs

Romaine, Venn, and Newton were all Calvinists; Fletcher was not, siding with the Arminian position of free will as espoused by Wesley. The Calvinism that Venn adopted was the classic Calvinism of Anglican evangelicalism: "As to Calvinism, I am a moderate,"[23] he reported in 1772. This was also reflected in his approach to others. He was asked to comment on whether he thought a young minister he knew was a Calvinist or an Arminian. He responded, "I really do not know; he is a sincere disciple of the Lord Jesus Christ; and that is of infinitely more importance than his being a disciple of Calvin or Arminius."[24] In 1763 Venn published his key Revival work, *The Complete Duty of Man*, though most of it was completed before his arrival in Huddersfield. A prominent anonymous work of Christian holiness had long circulated under the title *The Whole Duty of Man*, published in 1658 and representing the classic high-church holiness tradition. Venn sought to set out an evangelical perspective. The work was subtitled "A system of doctrinal and practical Christianity". He was clear in his preface where the distinction lay in his definition of saving faith: "I understand by it a dependence upon the righteousness and death of Christ, as a full satisfaction to the justice of God for the sin of the world… and the sole ground of our acceptance to the reward of eternal life."[25]

In 1765 Howell Harris personally asked John Fletcher to take up the presidency of Trevecca College, the training institution established by the Countess of Huntingdon. He met with the same response as Wesley: the Lord in his providence had placed him at Madeley. Yet in 1768, as we have already noted, he became president of Trevecca, although he remained the incumbent of his parish. He told Selina of his first impressions – the housekeeping bill was too high! The students, he noted, were making progress with both preaching and study, and he reported on each by name. In respect of one student, by the name of Cheek, however, he commented that "he hath not made those progress in his studies I expected not owing to want to Application but of Memory".[26] The split over the minutes of Wesley's Methodist Conference of 1770 led to his resignation. In September 1770 he wrote to Charles Wesley, noting, in respect of John, "the sadness caused me by the distance between Lady Huntingdon and him".[27] Writing to John Wesley in 1771, Fletcher said, "If every Arminian must quit the college, I am discharg'd for one, for I cannot give up the possibility of the salvation of all."[28] In March 1771 he wrote a lengthy letter to Selina, concluding with his resignation: "I should not act the part of an honest man if I did not absolutely resign my charge, and take leave of this seminary of pious learning."[29] His real and expressed worry was that the appointment of a Calvinist to the college would result in a loss of evangelistic zeal. During the years 1771–76 he wrote a series of tracts which collectively became known as "Checks to Antinomianism" – the title referring to the criticism of Calvinism that it led to a cavalier approach to Christian law and holiness. He viewed the American Revolutionaries as equally lawless and godless!

Romaine revealed his evangelicalism through an unswerving attachment to the Scriptures. After reading the Bible through in 1783 he remarked, "It has been a season of great teaching. I never went through it with more delight or with more profit. My soul has found it more precious than gold and it is really sweeter than honey."[30] He described the Bible as "the infallible standard of truth".[31] There are regular references in his correspondence to reading the Bible from end to end. These early divines preached so frequently that it is not surprising that their health gave way. Romaine's letters refer to twelve, eight, and seven times preaching in a week. He commented towards the end of his life, "It is better to burn out than to rust out."[32] Romaine was a Calvinist. He contrasted the crowning of free will with the debasing of King Jesus, and claimed he would not be an Arminian for the entire world.

> It is the proper work of the grace of Jesus, to humble the proud sinner, to make him and to keep him sensible of his wants, convinced always that he has not any good of his own, and cannot possibly of himself obtain any, either in earth or heaven...[33]

Romaine was scathing about his own earlier attraction to Arminianism (a common experience for many Revival clergy). He described the attraction as "sweet food to a proud heart", but the striving and the agonizing left him unsatisfied: "No galley slave worked harder." The outcome was his adoption of Calvinism, most importantly that "the benefits of salvation are all the free gifts of free grace, conferred without any regard to what the receiver of them is".[34]

In 1753 Romaine became embroiled in religious and political controversy surrounding the so-called "Jew Bill" – more precisely, the Jewish Naturalization Bill. This proposed to allow Jewish people born outside England to be naturalized without receiving the sacrament of the Lord's Supper, according to the rites of the Church of England. Within a year the Bill had passed through Parliament and was then repealed. At the heart of the controversy lay the classic ultra-Protestant claim that the country was a Christian nation and that constitutional requirements should reflect this. Parliamentary opposition to the Bill was led by the usual culprits, Lord Shaftesbury and Sir Robert Inglis. However, outside the hallowed courts of Westminster it was the pen of William Romaine that sought to give intellectual weight to opposition that was not restricted to, but certainly included, an anti-Jewish rabble. To the Bill's opponents, it was a slippery slope that could lead only to full constitutional rights for non-conformists and even Roman Catholics. Romaine was fierce in his opposition. The Jews, he argued, threatened order; after all they had rejected Christ and in effect were guilty of treason. This was hardly auspicious, but not uncommon among Established Church Protestants at the time.

Revival links

The real complexity of the Revival, and maybe part of its excitement, is that so many of its key players related to each other across many tensions and divides, both doctrinal and practical.

Numerous men came forward from Venn's Huddersfield ministry to offer themselves for ordination, though many stepped outside the Church of England to exercise that ministry. In 1767 his wife died. "Plead for me with our God and Saviour! He has made me very desolate: this day I am become a widower, and have lost as much as could be lost in the name of wife and mother,"[35] he wrote. Venn's own health was declining and in 1771 he accepted the less onerous rural parish of Yelling, near Huntingdon. Shortly afterwards, he remarried. He wrote to a Mrs Riland, "Nothing would have prevailed upon me to leave Huddersfield, if my lungs had not received an irreparable injury... I go to Yelling a dying man."[36] In fact he lived for another twenty-seven years, with a flourishing ministry. Within a few miles were two other evangelical clergy, John Newton at Olney and John Berridge at Everton. Apparently Venn had a weekly meeting with Berridge, who also regularly preached for him in Yelling; they were later joined by Charles Simeon. Simeon often walked to Yelling, and frequently stayed the night. Being close to Cambridge also meant that Venn's vicarage, like Simeon's later, became a venue for gatherings of students and, indeed, of young ministers, eager to receive counsel. In 1783 Venn predicted that "Mr Simeon's ministry is likely to be blessed... Many gownsmen hear him."[37] Unlike Simeon, both Venn and Berridge preached beyond their own parish – Venn often went on preaching tours for the Countess of Huntingdon. He described one such tour in 1766. He said he was "fired and encouraged by the example of Lady Huntingdon, and dear Mr. Fletcher" at Brighton – showing once again how relationships, albeit with their ups and downs, transcended much of the doctrinal debate that took place. He mentioned a visit to Pewsey, referring to the "dear minister", a Mr Townsend, as having "a single eye and a warm heart". He also noted speaking "the word of life to a small church-full", and "round about there are a great number of souls awakened". He then went to Bath, hearing William Romaine preach "in that most plain but elegant chapel of Lady Huntingdon".[38] On a subsequent visit there he illustrated the extraordinarily high regard in which the Revival pioneers held the Countess: "In Lady Huntingdon I see a star of the first magnitude in the firmament of the Church."[39] Following visits to Bristol and Gloucester, Venn then arrived in Trevecca and met Howell Harris. He saw itinerancy as a temporary expedient and resigned his chaplaincy to the Countess when her chapels were registered as dissenting meeting houses. Berridge, on the other hand, although he usually preached more locally in neighbouring parishes, did so more as a matter of principle.

Last days

As tension built within Methodism over its future relationship with the Church of England, John Fletcher pleaded for peace. In the early 1770s he consistently refused offers to be named as John Wesley's successor. John Fletcher died in 1785 and his wife Mary carried on their Shropshire ministry for the next thirty years, with curates, Methodist lay preachers, and all the normal paraphernalia of the Revival. As Forsaith notes, the consequence of this was that "Madeley was one of the last parishes where Methodism remained within the Church of England".[40]

Romaine preached his last sermons at St Dunstan's and Blackfriars in June 1795. He died on 26 July. A few days earlier he had remarked, "It is now near sixty years since God opened my mouth to publish the everlasting sufficiency and eternal glory of the salvation of Christ Jesus; and it has now pleased him to shut my mouth, that my heart might feel and experience what my mouth hath so often spoken."[41] His last words were, "He is a precious Saviour to me now."[42] He died at a friend's house in Balham Hill. As the funeral procession gathered on Clapham Common, some fifty coaches followed, and there were many others on foot. The Lord Mayor ordered the city marshals to accompany the funeral cortège as it entered the City. The funeral sermon was preached by the Revd William Goode, who was to carry the evangelical torch into the next century.

Simeon was fulsome in his praise of Venn: "I found a father, an instructor, and a most bright example; and I shall ever have reason to adore my God to all eternity for the benefit of his acquaintance."[43] Venn's great friend John Berridge died in 1793. The ministry in Yelling continued until six months before Venn's death in June 1797 at the age of seventy-three – at that point he had returned to Clapham, where his son John was now Rector, as the Revival moved into the heartlands of the Established Church of England.

Newton died on 21 December 1807, a few months after the Bill to abolish the slave trade had become the law of the land. His legacy is summed up in the famous memorial epitaph:

John Newton

Clerk

Once an infidel and libertine,

A servant of slaves in Africa,

Was,

By the rich mercy
of our Lord and Saviour
Jesus Christ,
Preserved, restored, pardoned
And appointed to preach the faith
He had long laboured to destroy...[44]

Many individuals helped the Countess of Huntingdon to consolidate the Revival, with the brothers Wesley and George Whitefield providing the glue that held it all together. Or *did* they? An alternative view is that it was in fact the practitioners on the ground that formed and shaped the Revival, with the more famous itinerants providing the icing on the cake. Many names could have been selected; the four chosen here illustrate how the Revival came to take root through dedicated work, albeit often generating opposition, in the middle decades of the century.

CHAPTER 8

The maturing of the Revival

Revivals, awakenings, outpourings – the explainable, and the unfathomable – are essentially movements. Hence they reflect a whirlpool of activism, powerful encounters, speed, and transformation. We see this in the theology – encounter with God, conversion – and the methodology – itinerancy and preaching in the open air. This phenomenon is also illustrated by individuals: Wesley on his horse, Grimshaw on the Haworth round. Revivals ultimately become institutionalized. The very movements of people that were once so radical become conservative protectors of the status quo. In turn, that generates new revival movements, and so the process continues. As we draw to the end of the eighteenth century we see this happening not only inside the Church of England but even in the radical movements outside the Established Church. This Revival – for better or worse, and like every other example – matured.

The Established Church

The evangelicals in the Church of England became, slowly but surely, more established, and indeed more establishment. London became more congenial territory for evangelicals, helped by William Wilberforce's foray into public policy. The pattern for the future of evangelicalism within the Established Church in the closing decades of the eighteenth and early years of the nineteenth century is perhaps best illustrated by Charles Simeon. Simeon was deeply influential, though he became less radical over time and by the end of his ministry represented a sort of moderate evangelicalism that was soon out of step with both the early fathers of evangelicalism and its passionate adherents in the 1820s. The title "Prince of Evangelicals"[1] is perhaps overstated.

Born in 1759, as many of the pioneers were consolidating the Revival in the parishes and circuits of England, Simeon belonged to a different generation. Like so many of those who went before him (and indeed who came after), Simeon went through a conversion experience, in his case in the chapel of King's College, Cambridge, in 1779. Proceeding to a Fellowship and to ordination, he was finally appointed minister of Holy Trinity, Cambridge, in 1782. He faced many of the challenges and opportunities of the early revival preachers. There was opposition from within the Church and also from the university. Yet Simeon painstakingly persevered with his meetings for tea and conversation and, of course, his famous sermon classes. Simeon produced 600 skeletal sermons. He was involved in the Eclectic Society and, in 1799, as our narrative closes, in the foundation of the Church Missionary Society. His doctrine was the classic moderate Calvinism of the Church of England, based on the centrality of Scripture and the cross. His view of the Bible was that it carried its own authority and the reader was not to seek to impose any system on Scripture, either Calvinist or Arminian, but to "bring out of scripture what is there, and not to thrust in what I think might be there".[2] Simeon was also utterly attached to the liturgical formulations of the Book of Common Prayer and to the principle of the establishment of the Church; indeed, he took this to extremes. His only adventures outside the Church of England were when he was in Scotland, where he attended the Church of Scotland because that was the established church of that land. Indeed, he even preached in a Presbyterian pulpit![3] Some scholars claim that it was Simeon's influence that kept the evangelical clergy in the Church of England.[4] This is an overstatement. Simeon was a significant second-generation evangelical leader who, partially through his own convictions but also through the developing context of evangelical witness in the Church of England, contributed to a firmly rooted presence in the Established Church. He was ambiguous in his attitude to dissent, but in essence regarded it as evil in principle, reinforced by his respect for parish boundaries. The attachment to the Church of England was partially pragmatic, but also theologically he saw the parochial system as the best means of ensuring a Christian society. Hence, despite the conflicts, the opposition, and the challenges, Simeon was a key figure in articulating and representing an evangelical view that grounded evangelicalism within the order of the Church of England.

Evangelicalism was also becoming more respectable within the Established Church. William Wilberforce's campaign against the slave trade brought evangelical witness into the public and the social square. The movement may also have become more bourgeois. Voluntary societies were formed, Sunday schools established, and missionary societies founded. The evangelical gospel still reached the upper classes. Hannah More (1745–1833) was not of the same aristocratic stock as Lady Huntingdon, but she was none the less a prominent figure as the Revival matured. Henry Venn was, as we noted, curate of Clapham. The village, as it then was, became famous. Wilberforce's campaign against the slave trade brought him into contact with other prominent abolitionists. John Thornton was already living in Clapham when Venn was minister, and Wilberforce later spent time at his house and grew close to one of his sons. Henry Thornton became a wealthy banker and it was on his estate in Clapham that these friends began to buy houses: from around 1792, Wilberforce, Thomas Babington, Zachary Macaulay, James Stephen, Lord Teignmouth, Charles Grant, and others all took up residence. The numbers varied over the years and there was a good deal of intermarriage in the families concerned. However, at its core this group became the heartbeat of a maturing evangelicalism. Clapham provided a base for philanthropy, theological discussion, spiritual growth, and development.

Wilberforce published an influential book – *A Practical View of the Prevailing Religious System of Professed Christians in the Higher and Middle Classes in this Country Contrasted with Real Christianity*. The lengthy title illustrated what was going on. The book was a roaring success in publishing terms – by 1837 there had been fifteen editions and 75,000 copies sold, figures published historians today can only dream of. The book had weight. It dealt with practical divinity of the heart. It set out in classic Calvinist terms the all-pervading nature of sin. Wilberforce wrote:

> ...man is an apostate creature, fallen from his high
> original, degraded in his nature, and depraved in his
> faculties; indisposed to good, and disposed to evil;
> prone to vice, it is natural and easy to him; disinclined
> to virtue, it is difficult and laborious; that he is tainted
> with sin, not slightly and superficially, but radically and
> to the very core.[5]

Wilberforce protested eloquently against the compart-mentalization of religion; faith was an all-consuming passion. Yet the book – known simply as *A Practical View* – also revealed that evangelicalism was in danger of being adopted by a middle-class elite as well as bringing the challenge of a transforming faith into its heart. There was an allegation that evangelicals were only concerned with the morals of the poor.

The failure of the London Missionary Society (LMS), founded in 1795, to encapsulate a renewed evangelical vision also revealed the changing nature of evangelicalism as the century of revival came to a close. The society was interdenominational. The crossing of denominational boundaries was commonplace in the early years of the Revival, and would become so again in the middle decades of the nineteenth century. Somehow, though, the 1790s and early decades of the nineteenth century did not seem to be quite the right time. Evangelicals in the Established Church generally declined to support the LMS and responded with the foundation of the Church Missionary Society (CMS) in 1799. William Carey had founded the Baptist Missionary Society in 1792, but with LMS the issue for most members of the Church of England was, once again, that of church order. It was all very well to convert the heathen, but what form of church government would the converts be introduced to? This was a question sixty years or so after the Revival began, not one that concerned the early participants, certainly not beyond the matter of parish boundaries. So it was that members of the Established Church founded The Society for Missions to Africa and the East, later known as the Church Missionary Society. The establishment of CMS illustrated that the Protestant impulse to mission remained alive and well within the Church of England. However, that very impetus was now institutionalized. One might even argue that the next period of evangelical history was indeed that of societies and institutions. The future leader of nineteenth-century evangelicalism, Anthony Ashley Cooper, later the seventh Earl of Shaftesbury, was born in 1801. His story belongs elsewhere.[6]

Methodism

Outside the Established Church, factors were at work that led to the formal establishment of Methodism. The Revival was being institutionalized both within and without the Church of England. Wesley had been gathering together his lay preachers in the annual Conference since 1744. As time went on the question that emerged for him was how to ensure the continuation of his work after his death. The same question exercised many of the Revival leaders; Wesley had done the most to prepare a response, and his answer had profound implications. He recognized the need to make longer-term provision for the oversight of the lay preachers and religious societies after his death. He had nominated John Fletcher to be his successor, but Fletcher's health was not up to it; in fact it was Wesley who preached the sermon at Fletcher's funeral in 1785.

In February 1784 Wesley drew up the "Legal Hundred", the name given to a document that set down how the Methodist Conference was to operate after his death. The deed stipulated that 100 people be called to the Conference – the Legal Hundred. There were rules for the conduct of the Conference, its regularity (annual), and length of meeting (not less than five days, nor more than three weeks), and there were also rules for the appointment of preachers to the Methodist chapels. There were at this point 191 Methodist preachers; only a hundred were appointed to the Conference (against the advice of Thomas Coke), and five resigned in protest. The organization of the Legal Hundred was, however, designed to keep Methodism within the boundaries and framework of the Church of England: preachers were to be members of or connected to the Conference, or ordained in the Church of England. Until the challenge of providing for the ministry across the Atlantic arose, Wesley did nothing to place his societies or his preachers outside the Established Church. However, the strength of the bonds within his movement, both personal and organizational, probably made this an unrealistic longer-term proposition.

A more serious concern was how to ensure the continuation of the American ministry. Methodism had grown rapidly in the 1770s and Wesley was unsuccessful in persuading the Bishop of London to ordain workers for the task. Francis Asbury, already in America as one of Wesley's lay preachers, told him that many problems ensued from this – there were many unbaptized individuals and similarly significant numbers who did not have the opportunity to share in the Lord's Supper. Wesley concluded that he must act, and did so, in Bristol in 1784. He saw the provision of ministry for souls as a gospel imperative which superseded the demands of church order. Hence, three men – Thomas Coke on one day, followed by Richard Whatcoat and Thomas Vasey the next day – were ordained by Wesley for the work in America. He noted that in America there were no ministers for hundreds of miles apart: "There is none either to baptise, or to administer the Lord's Supper." He went on:

> Here, therefore, my scruples are at an end, and I conceive myself at full liberty, as I violate no order and invade no man's right by appointing and sending labourers into the harvest... [7]

Wesley had long resisted earlier calls for such provision in various places, relying mainly on his argument of the availability of ministry in the parish churches. This was not the case in America. In his *Journal*, Wesley was matter of fact – "Being now clear in my own mind, I took a step which I had long weighed in my mind, and appointed Mr Whatcoat and Mr Vasey to go and serve the desolate sheep in America." [8] In his diary he refers to "ordination". The certificate of ordination for Thomas Coke sets out both the basis and the rationale. Wesley, describing himself as a "presbyter of the Church of England", and noting that many of those in North America "desire to continue under my care" but adhere to "the doctrines and discipline of the Church of England", notes the lack of ministers and then adds:

> Know all men that I, John Wesley, think myself to be providentially called at this time to set apart some persons for the work of the ministry in America. And

therefore under the protection of Almighty God, and with a single eye to his glory, I have this day set apart as a superintendent, by the imposition of my hands and prayer (being assisted by other ordained ministers), Thomas Coke, Doctor of Civil Laws and Presbyter of the Church of England, a man whom I judge to be well qualified for that great work.[9]

The assisting minister was James Creighton. Coke was empowered to conduct ordinations – a step that went considerably further than the itinerancy and field preaching across England and America. Wesley was not simply breaching accepted practice; he was, especially by investing Coke with powers of ordination, rewriting church order. He continued his preaching tour as if nothing out of the ordinary had occurred. The outcome was probably inevitable, even though Wesley sent them out with a liturgy little different from that of the Church of England. In frontier America the Methodist chapels were soon asserting their independence and, to Wesley's chagrin, Francis Asbury and Thomas Coke began to call themselves bishops. Wesley protested, but to no avail. He really should not have been surprised. The more moderate Charles Wesley was deeply upset and disturbed by the move. The two brothers argued in correspondence but remained friends. There is a famous poem by Charles:

So easily are Bishops made,
By man's, or woman's whim?
W– his hands on C– hath laid,
But who laid hands on him?[10]

John followed up his first move by ordaining three preachers for Scotland in 1785 and one for service in England in 1788. Charles continued to protest, describing the Methodists as nothing more than "a new sect of Presbyterians".[11] However, his health was failing. He died on 29 March 1788, requesting burial in the churchyard of St Marylebone Parish Church since he had lived and died a communicant member of the Church of England. John had just a few years to live, although his activity did not seem to lessen. In June 1790 he wrote to the Bishop of Lincoln urging him not to force the Methodists out of the Church. He died on 2 March 1791. Unlike Charles, he was buried beside a Methodist chapel. Three months later the Countess of Huntingdon died. Both Wesleyan and Calvinist branches of the Revival were on the way to being organized outside the Established Church, against the wishes of their founders. For both these movements the imperatives of the gospel triumphed over church order. The debate continued after John Wesley's death. In 1792 preachers in three areas voted to remain within the Church of England, but in at least one other the decision was to offer the Supper in the context of the religious societies, a clear move of separation. This policy was sanctioned by the 1793 Conference. In 1795 the Plan of Pacification failed to placate, and enshrined the right to receive the sacrament of the Supper if a majority of the local leadership favoured such a move.

It is estimated that by 1790 there were 55,000 Methodists connected to the societies. Although the tension continued for some time, by 1795 Methodism was effectively established as a separate and distinctive denomination. Things went at a slower pace in Wales, where it was as late as 1810–11 that the Calvinistic Methodist Connexion in Wales also began to conduct its own ordinations. In this first decade of the new century there were some nineteen clergy of the Established Church still serving the Connexion.

Perhaps a good way to conclude our survey is to note the emergence in 1807 of the new radicals. Field preaching, the proclamation of the new birth, and the accompanying complexities of prophecies and phenomena seemed a long way away, even though only some sixty years had passed since Wesley and Whitefield began their open-air campaigns. Those who continued to advocate a radical edge to the proclamation of Revival soon became unacceptable to the new Methodist establishment. Lengthy gatherings of large numbers for prayer, praise, and preaching with maybe a hint of disorderly trances and so on were too much to bear. What was more, the leadership was tainted not only with extreme millennialism but also with republicanism and political radicalism. Today's Methodists may not be Tories, but their predecessors certainly were! The best-known event was the gathering (a prayer meeting) on Mow Cop, a rocky outcrop in Staffordshire, on 31 May 1807. The camp meetings were condemned and discipline was imposed. Their two early leaders, Hugh Bourne and William Clowes, were expelled from the Wesleyan Methodist Connexion in 1808 and 1810 respectively. So began the Primitive Methodist Connexion – more radical, less establishment, appealing to the poor, empowering women. The full history does not belong here, but the emergence of Primitive Methodism illustrates how the Revival both matured and was then once again radicalized, though certainly not with the same dynamism we saw in Wesley and Whitefield and the pioneers that followed them.

Conclusion

Mark Noll, in his summary of the Revival in his splendid book *The Rise of Evangelicalism,* sums up the position thus:

> Evangelicalism was never static or simply given. Right from the start, the energy that brought that movement into existence pushed on to further innovations, expanded the depth and breadth of its reach, suffered from countless mis-steps, divided into hotly competing fragments and entered into ever-new connections with the broader society. Always at the centre was engagement with the gospel. And the years from 1740 to 1795 were only the beginning.[1]

Mr Grimshaw and Mr Wilberforce lived in different ages, albeit separated by only fifty years or so. To William Grimshaw and the other pioneers, the gospel was the imperative: teaching it in cottages to small groups, proclaiming it from pulpits and fields to large crowds. The gospel was for the poor and for the aristocracy. Nothing else mattered. For most of the pioneers, most of the time, the things that did not matter included parochial boundaries and church order. Wesley and Whitefield were driven by this imperative. They too had doctrinal disputes, some of which were very serious and unquestionably damaged the Revival's expansion. The methods were innovative, the participants enormously creative. Friendships were formed, maintained, and sometimes broken. The story itself is quite simply exciting. There was the constant pressure of opposition, sometimes from those who were meant to be the public representatives of the faith being proclaimed. Naturally, the early pioneers rather enjoyed the opposition. They stood firm. By the end of the century the Evangelical Revival had made significant steps forward; the gospel was being set forth at the heart of society and its governance. Yet, at the same time, something of the creativity, the raw passion, and the pioneering spirit was lost. New institutions were established and some older ones revitalized.

There are many aspects to an explanation of the origins of the Evangelical Revival. However, it is clear from the story that not only to its participants was it a work of God, but even to the dispassionate observer much was happening that was simply unexplainable in any other coherent way. John Wesley was a towering figure. Perhaps not the best individual to give marriage advice (Charles was a better option there), but he transformed both religion and society through his extraordinary organizational skills and abilities, the personal oversight he gave to the religious societies, and the structure he established. The development of Methodism as an institution rather than a movement was probably inevitable; John would have lamented the necessity and remained ordained in the Church of England. He would still have been driven by the necessity of the gospel and done whatever was needed to ensure that the message was spread. Charles would have continued to write wonderful hymns.

Those hymns, enjoyed by so many today, were of course deeply polemical at the time, with many hints of anti-Calvinism and suggestions of perfectionism. The irony is that those at whom they were aimed, the likes of George Whitefield and Selina, Countess of Huntingdon, are potentially more important for the Revival and its understanding than the Wesleys. Whitefield represented the classic moderate Calvinism of the Established Church. However, he spent too long in the colonies to be effective and died too early – twenty-one years before John Wesley. The Wesleyan legacy is the one that is remembered. The doctrines of Whitefield, Grimshaw, Venn, Romaine, and Newton were in direct continuity with those of the Protestant Reformation. Those doctrines were secured for the Established Church, but fared less well outside it. The Wesleyan free-will position could ultimately be maintained only outside the Church of England. So Whitefield may be less known, but his influence is arguably more determinative even than Wesley's.

The methods of the Revival brought new life to the message of new birth. The Revival spread not only across the English-speaking world but far beyond. Will England ever see such a phenomenon again? Well, you never know.

Appendix

Approaches to the Revival

People use a variety of approaches to study the Revival. The phenomenon may be viewed as social, cultural, or religious history, and varying emphasis can be given to psychological, class, or political factors. Historians writing from a Christian perspective may seek explanations that view God as intervening directly in human affairs – the "providential" view of history. God has acted – unless, of course, the historian does not believe in God. Secular historians of the eighteenth century tend to be dismissive of the providential view. Indeed, some deny the existence of anything characterized as an Evangelical Revival. However, there may be factors that other approaches to history cannot explain. Christian historians, although correct in addressing the question of providence, can also overplay their hand. If the Revival or Awakening was a work of God, other aspects too play a part in any assessment of its causes and origins. What can be demonstrated, however, is that the history of the Revival forms part not just of social, cultural, or even ecclesiastical history but also of the history of ideas. Many elements formed the background to the Revival, but it cannot be explained simply in phenomenological terms. Even the rather unholy battles between Wesley and Whitefield had at their root a contest for Protestantism. The Christian historian has a responsibility to assess the whole range of factors that lie behind the outbreak of Revival and Awakening, including religious, political, and social aspects. As John Walsh explains, "The origins of the Revival can be examined on different – though not irreconcilable – levels."[1] Walsh refers to political, doctrinal, ecclesiastical, psychological, social, and economic factors, but also "as the evangelicals themselves saw it, as the providential effusion of the Holy Spirit in the national life".[2] The secular historian needs, however, to recognize that not all elements can be explained in socio-cultural terms and that there remains an element of the unexplained.

David Bebbington has posed for historians a further question which is of significance in assessing how we are to understand the history of the Revival. When did evangelicalism begin? Evangelicalism – as a defined group of believers with certain doctrines and emphases and with a significant subsequent history within and without the Church of England – clearly derives from the Evangelical Revival. However, David Bebbington's portrayal of the phenomenon as "a popular Protestant movement that has existed in Britain since the 1730s"[3] does raise several questions. Bebbington, for a variety of reasons, emphasizes something of the "newness" of the phenomenon of the Revival. In this he gives weight to the discontinuities with what had previously passed as Protestantism – the Reformation, both continental and in Great Britain, represented by theologies such as Calvinism and movements like Puritanism. There are good reasons for him to adopt this approach. There were, as has been described, some new, even unique, features to this particular outbreak of popular religion and faith. Indeed, although field preaching and itinerancy were not entirely novel, Whitefield and others became what Bebbington refers to as "star personalities in a way that was alien to an earlier age".[4] Bebbington goes further and argues that the consequence of conversion – the assurance of salvation – was, in fact, a turning on the head of the classic lack of assurance which was reflected in the daily Puritan struggle against sin, though this may be a confusion of categories and some, at least, would contest the assertion. In other words, Bebbington argues that not only in method but also in some aspects of doctrine and belief, there was considerable discontinuity with the past. Certainly there had been nothing on the scale of the Revival before and many of its emphases and methods were innovative. However, Bebbington may also be overplaying his hand. His analysis can leave the impression that evangelicalism emerged out of nothing; this was clearly not the case, and Bebbington does not in reality believe it to be so.[5] There was continuity with what had gone before. The evangelicalism of the Revival was not entirely new. The doctrinal emphases on sin, depravity, and justification were key themes in the Protestant heritage of the Reformation. Bebbington's great achievement was to set evangelicalism and its emergence in the Revival within the wider context of cultural trends and intellectual currents. However, he may have given insufficient weight to the ways in which it influenced society and culture as well as being shaped by it.

Religion in England before the Revival

Several commentators, including Gordon Rupp and Jonathan Clark, have drawn attention to the continuing influence of religion and faith in society in the period 1688–1738. Bill

Jacob chimes in, suggesting that in this "long eighteenth century religion was central in people's lives, individually and collectively, in local communities and nationally".[6] The correction is important and necessary. However, what exactly *was* this religion that held the nation together?

Gordon Rupp's survey reminds us that, rather than the classic bleak and gloomy picture, the period was full of religion not empty of it. Whether it was full of faith is a different matter. There was a great deal of variety: Quakers, non-jurors, deists, high church, dissenters of one type or another, and, of course, good old Church of England men. Rupp's volume extends, conveniently, to 1791; there might have been a good deal less material if it had concluded fifty years earlier. The variety illustrates the problem. It is not, as some may suggest, that there was no religious faith or piety in the period before the Revival, but that it had lost its coherence. There was now no overarching narrative, and a degree of quietism would be hard to deny.

If Gordon Rupp represents the infantry, gradually retaking the ground for at least one form of revisionist scholarship, then Jonathan Clark represents the cavalry, charging ahead to reclaim the half-century after William and Mary for the Church and for religion. Clark's analysis extends to 1832 and provides a welcome challenge to much modernist, revisionist, progressive history. Clark's book, *English Society 1660–1832*, is concerned with the nature and understanding of society between the Restoration and the Reform Act. Religion clearly formed a significant element of the fabric of society. Clark argues for the coherence of the structure of society, including the religious. In rejecting what he describes as the polarities of the nineteenth century he appeals to the middle ground by rejecting pejorative labels. So:

> ...we increasingly appreciate the significance of the middle ground of English life: that social form which presented itself as both constitutional *and* royalist, libertarian *and* stable, tolerant *and* expressing religious orthodoxy, innovative *and* respectful of what was customary.[7]

Here lies the problem. The early historians of the Revival had overstated their case. They had tended to dismiss all that had gone before, emphasizing the discontinuity of the Revival with the previous structures of society and religion. The corrective is now in place. However, it would be very hard to deny that there was a loss, not just of momentum but of substance, in what would later be known as "vital" religion. Some may have feared popery; many more were alarmed that the settlement of 1688 put the church at risk from "dissent". There were significant moves in the latter years of the seventeenth century to strengthen the Church institutionally in respect of order, discipline, and control. Religion was certainly not lacking; indeed the middle way was being imposed. Walsh notes that the

> sermons of the 1720s, 1740s and 1750s are predominately (if safely) controversial (against Deists, Papists or Enthusiasts) or ethical (concerned with philanthropic enterprises like the charity schools) or sonorously pastoral. They offer to the layman little clear-cut, dogmatic content. They speak little to the soul concerned with the great themes of sin and salvation....[8]

Britain was viewed as a coherent, meaningful Protestant nation; this faith was the very basis of national life, indeed of the relationship of Church and state. However, as Mark Noll has commented, neither "active personal piety nor conscientious holy living was necessarily the consequence of holding these assumptions, but as assumptions they did not begin to give way for a long time".[9]

The influence of continental Pietism

Pietism is crucial to the background of the Revival. The historian of the international dimensions of the Revival, Professor W. R. Ward, claims that it was the influence of continental Pietism that prepared the British churches to be receptive to news of Revival in the American colonies.[10] It is an important point. However, to understand it we need to investigate further the background and nature of Pietism. Unsurprisingly, Pietism and its origins are complex matters. The background lies in the post-Reformation religious diversity in continental Europe, especially in the United Provinces (the Netherlands) and the Spanish Netherlands (Belgium), together with the importance attached to religious experience that had emerged in what was known as the Radical Reformation. This emphasis on experience and the inner life of faith was mediated through elements of both Reformed and Lutheran churches and came to form and shape Pietism. A key figure in its early development was Philipp Jakob Spener (1635–1705), who was influenced by Johann Arndt (1555–1621). It was Arndt who stressed the place of transformation of the heart, mind, and affections.[11] Two aspects of Spener's development are relevant. In 1666 he was appointed senior pastor over all the Lutheran ministers in Frankfurt. He advocated small-group meetings for the purposes of spiritual edification. These gatherings were known as *collegia pietatis* – "gatherings for piety". They were reminiscent of "preachers' gatherings" – the conventicles of the Puritan era and thereafter; we see here also the forerunner of Wesley's Methodist classes and bands. In 1675 Spener published *Pia Desideria,* effectively his manifesto for church reform. The audience was not just clergy but the whole people of God, with a call to Scripture, love, and piety. His work provoked opposition on the grounds that it threatened good order; the spiritual analysis, however, was sound. The name applied to this movement, "Pietists", emerged in the 1680s as a term of abuse rather than endearment.

Another name to note was that of August Hermann Francke (1663–1727). In 1687 Francke underwent a conversion experience: "I was sure in my heart of the grace of God in Jesus Christ; I knew God not only as God, but rather as one called my Father."[12] Pietistic leanings in the Lutheran Church were generally less than welcome. Francke allied himself with Spener and, prevented from lecturing in Leipzig, he moved to what became the key place in the development of Pietism, the University of Halle. As Ted Campbell notes, Francke "built a kind of pietistic empire in Halle, and he was to dominate the city and the University for the next three decades".[13] A variety of institutions emerged there: schools and educational institutes, publishing houses, and, perhaps most famously, an orphanage. The religion of the heart had practical consequences. Theologically the emerging Pietist movement departed from the traditional Calvinist categories of election and predestination and indeed from the sacramental understanding of baptism as the outward sign of a regenerate heart; for the Pietist, new birth was required. The movement spread in influence across Europe, not least in countries where Catholicism exercised not just a heavy but indeed an oppressive hand.

Explaining the Revival

Walsh, in his classic grouping of explanations (high-church piety, continuing Puritan tradition, reaction against rationalism), rightly draws attention to some of the multifarious factors and influences that lie behind the Revival and which have influenced scholars for many years. Scholarship has moved on since then. The problem with Walsh's original essay is that it leaves the impression that the Revival came about as a result of some sort of combination of these factors. This is a classic synthesis of arguments that on their own cannot make the case. The case that remains is itself inadequate, but before we seek to draw conclusions about the origins and sources of the Revival there remains one crucial aspect of recent scholarship to consider.

The international dimension

The major aspect of scholarship on the Revival's origins since Walsh's article has been much greater recognition and weight being given to international dimensions. Walsh acknowledged in 1994 that until "very recently the evangelical awakenings of the 1730s and 1740s were treated as events in splendid isolation".[14] He added that the occurrences are "now being treated in terms of comparative history not merely as regional events but as constituent elements of an international and pan-Protestant phenomenon".[15] This is an important corrective. There are a number of aspects as well as consequences.

The two international elements of particular relevance are, first, influences from the continent of Europe and, second, transatlantic connections. These links opened up channels of communication, through which flowed news and reports about revival and personal bonds between individual participants. In addition, both immigration and the movement of refugees prompted concern for the victims of European Catholicism. The role of Pietism in central Europe was of particular importance, as noted by Noll, who adds into the mix "the Pietist revival from the European continent".[16]

The influence of Pietism is undeniable and some of the encounters between the Wesleys and the Moravians were crucial for their own spiritual development and that of the English Evangelical Revival. The recognition of these influences as part of the background to the Revival is significant. However, we should also be careful not to attribute too much influence to the Moravian and Pietistic element. Pietism was essentially a renewal movement within continental Lutheranism rather than a revival in itself. It embraced elements of theology that were central to the Revival but also some mystical emphases and practices from Catholicism that were far removed from traditional Calvinism. There were complex divisions between the main protagonists both before and after the Revival. The promotion of inner godliness, hymnody, personal encounter, and new birth was deeply influential on the Revival. There were common convictions, albeit a different social, cultural, and ecclesial context. Some of the theological emphases within Pietism ("the wounds of Jesus", "quietness or stillness") did not sit well with an England where Calvinism and Puritanism remained formative for the national Church; revival in England was, at least in part, likely to reflect some of this context.

Persecution and immigration were other factors from continental Europe that provided a conduit for Revival. Austrian persecution culminated in November 1731 in the expulsion of all Protestants over the age of twelve from Salzburg. Those under twelve were placed with Catholic foster parents. A mere eight days' notice was given. Ward describes the events as "one of the sensations of the eighteenth century".[17] The Protestants upped and went, on an unpredicted and unprecedented scale. The Protestant powers moved to protect the Salzburgers; finance was contributed, including by England, and the emigrants settled and were provided for – the largest group of 20,000 going to Prussia. Some ended up in the New World. The story travelled. It was said to be nothing short of a miracle – expelled for the sake of the gospel. The movement of Protestants around Europe contributed to the Revival. It stirred hearts and spread the increasing occurrences of conversion and new birth. It also began to encourage the circulation of stories of conversion. Although some Salzburgers eventually ended up in England (having left the Netherlands in search of pastoral oversight), it was Huguenot congregations that provided the most direct European Protestant link to England. They too had escaped from persecution over many generations, and a number were well established in London. They were receptive to the message of new birth and flooded into the religious societies. The Evangelical Revival in England cannot be considered in splendid isolation from Europe; the routes of influence were many and varied, and deeply significant.

Select bibliography

Aitken, J., *John Newton*, Wheaton, IL: Crossway, 2007.

Balleine, G. R., *A History of the Evangelical Party in the Church of England*, London: Longmans, Green & Co., 1908.

Bebbington, D. W., *Evangelicalism in Modern Britain,* London: Unwin Hyman, 1989.

Best, G., *Charles Wesley,* Peterborough: Epworth Press, 2006.

Campbell, Ted. A., *The Religion of the Heart*, University of South Carolina Press, 1991.

Clark, J. C. D., *English Society, 1660–1832,* Cambridge: CUP, second edition, 2000.

Cook, F., *William Grimshaw of Haworth,* Edinburgh: The Banner of Truth Trust, 1997.

Cook, F., *Selina, Countess of Huntingdon*, Edinburgh: Banner of Truth Trust, 2001.

Dallimore, A. A., *George Whitefield,* 2 volumes, London: Banner of Truth Trust, 1970.

Forsaith, Peter S. (ed.), *Unexampled Labours,* Peterborough: Epworth Press, 2008.

Harding, A., *Selina, Countess of Huntingdon,* Peterborough: Epworth Press, 2007.

Haykin, M. A. G., and Stewart, K. (eds), *The Emergence of Evangelicalism,* Nottingham: Apollos, 2008.

Hennell, M. M., *Henry Venn of Huddersfield*, Churchman, 068/2, 1954.

Hennell, M. M. & Pollard, A. (eds), *Charles Simeon 1759–1836,* London: SPCK, 1959.

Hindmarsh, D. Bruce, *The Evangelical Conversion Narrative,* Oxford: OUP, 2005.

Jacob, W. M., *The Clerical Profession in the Long Eighteenth Century, 1680–1840,* Oxford: OUP, 2007.

Kidd, T. S., *The Great Awakening,* New Haven and London: Yale University Press, 2007.

Lloyd-Jones, D. M., *The Puritans,* Edinburgh: Banner of Truth Trust, 1987.

Noll, M. A., *The Rise of Evangelicalism,* Leicester: IVP, 2004.

Noll, M. A., Bebbington, D. W. and Rawlyk, G. A., *Evangelicalism*, New York: OUP, 1994.

Rack, Henry, *Reasonable Enthusiast,* third edition, Peterborough: Epworth Press, 2002.

Romaine, W., *Works*, Edinburgh: T. Nelson, 1840.

Ryle, J. C., *Five Christian Leaders of the Eighteenth Century*, London: Charles J. Thynne, 1902.

Shenton, T., *A Cornish Revival,* Darlington: Evangelical Press, 2003.

Stout, H., *The Divine Dramatist*, Grand Rapids, MI: Eerdmans, 1991 (reprinted 1994).

Turnbull, R. D., *Shaftesbury: The Great Reformer,* Oxford: Lion Hudson, 2010.

Venn, H., *Letters of Henry Venn,* Edinburgh: Banner of Truth Trust, 1993.

Waller, R., *John Wesley, A Personal Portrait*, London: SPCK, 2003.

Walsh, J. D., "Origins of the Evangelical Revival", in G. V. Bennett and J. D. Walsh (eds), *Essays in Modern Church History,* New York: A & C Black, 1966.

Ward, W. R., The *Protestant Evangelical Awakening,* Cambridge: CUP, 1992.

Watts, M., *The Dissenters,* Oxford: Clarendon Press, 1978.

Wesley, J., *Journal of John Wesley,* standard edition, edited by Curnock, N., 8 volumes, London: Epworth Press, 1911, republished 1938.

Whitefield, G., *Journal,* George Whitefield's Journals, Edinburgh: Banner of Truth Trust, 1980.

Notes

Chapter 1: The origins of the Evangelical Revival

1. Bruce Hindmarsh, *The Evangelical Conversion Narrative,* Oxford: OUP, 2005, chapter 2.

2. M. Noll, *The Rise of Evangelicalism,* Leicester: IVP, 2004, page 15.

3. T. S. Kidd, *The Great Awakening,* New Haven and London: Yale University Press, 2007, page xiv.

4. J. D. Walsh, "'Methodism' and the origins of English-speaking Evangelicalism", in M. A. Noll, D. W. Bebbington and G. A. Rawlyk, *Evangelicalism,* New York: OUP, 1994, page 19.

5. Ted A. Campbell, *The Religion of the Heart*, University of South Carolina Press, 1991, page 111.

6. Ibid.

7. G. R. Balleine, *A History of the Evangelical Party in the Church of England*, London: Longmans, Green & Co., 1908, pages 12–16.

8. Ibid., page 21.

9. J. D. Walsh, "Origins of the Evangelical Revival", in G. V. Bennett and J. D. Walsh (eds), *Essays in Modern Church History,* New York: A & C Black, 1966, page 138.

10. J. Wesley, *Works*, vii, 9–10 (Sermon on Salvation by Faith), in Walsh, "Origins", page 149.

11. M. A. G. Haykin, in Michael Haykin and Kenneth Stewart (eds), *The Emergence of Evangelicalism,* Nottingham: Apollos, 2008, pages 18–19.

Chapter 2: The rectory and the inn

1. R. Waller, *John Wesley, A Personal Portrait*, London: SPCK, 2003, page 10.

2. Wesley, *Journal*, IV, page 90, quoted in Henry D. Rack, *Reasonable Enthusiast*, Peterborough: Epworth Press, 2002, page 533.

3. Rack, page 514.

4. "Further Thoughts on Separation from the Church," *Works*, xiii, 240.

5. H. Stout, *The Divine Dramatist*, Grand Rapids, MI: Eerdmans, 1991 (reprinted 1994).

6. Henry Rack, *Reasonable Enthusiast*, pages 48–49, quoting Adam Clarke, *Memoirs of the Wesley Family*, volume 1, London, 1836, page 198.

7. Letter from Susanna to Samuel Wesley, 6 February 1712, recorded in Curnock, *Journal of John Wesley*, volume 3, 1 August 1742, page 33.

8. Ibid.

9. Curnock, *Journal*, volume 3, page 34.

10. Ibid., page 35.

11. Ibid., page 37.

12. *George Whitefield's Journals*, Edinburgh: Banner of Truth Trust, 1960, "A Short Account", page 37.

13. Ibid., page 38.

14. Ibid., page 39.

15. Ibid.

16. Ibid., page 40.

17. Ibid.

18. Ibid., pages 40–41.

19. Ibid., page 43.

20. Waller, *Wesley*, page 16.

21. Rack, *Reasonable Enthusiast*, page 71.

22. Curnock, *Journal*, volume 1, page 59.

23. Rack, *Reasonable Enthusiast*, page 79.

24. Curnock, *Journal*, volume 1, page 51.

25. Ibid., pages 87ff.

26. Ibid., page 90.

27. Rack, *Reasonable Enthusiast,* page 84.

28. Whitefield, *Journals,* page 46.

29. Ibid.

30. Ibid., page 47.

31. Ibid., page 48.

32. Rack, *Reasonable Enthusiast,* page 111.

33. Curnock, *Journal,* volume 1, Sunday 25 January 1736, pages 141–42.

34. Ibid., page 142.

35. Ibid.

36. Ibid., pages 146–49.

37. Ibid., pages 213–14.

38. Letter to Charles Wesley, 22 March 1736.

39. Rack, *Reasonable Enthusiast,* page 126.

40. Curnock, *Journal,* volume 1, 29 November 1736.

41. Curnock, *Journal,* volume 1, 1 November 1736, page 294.

42. Curnock, *Journal,* volume 1, 8 February 1737, page 317

43. Rack, *Reasonable Enthusiast,* page 127.

Chapter 3: Preaching the new birth

1. Thomas Kidd, *The Great Awakening,* page 1.

2. Unpublished letter, 30 May 1735, quoted by Noll, *Rise of Evangelicalism,* page 70.

3. Whitefield, *Journals,* page 52.

4. Ibid., page 58.

5. A. A. Dallimore, *George Whitefield,* volume 1, London: Banner of Trust Trust, 1970, page 77.

6. R. Bennett, *The Early Years of Howell Harris*, Edinburgh: Banner of Truth Trust, 1909, pages 15–16.

7. Campbell, *Religion of the Heart*, page 103.

8. D. M. Lloyd-Jones, *The Puritans,* Edinburgh: Banner of Truth Trust, 1987, page 290.

9. Noll, *Rise of Evangelicalism*, page 73.

10. Campbell, *Religion of the Heart*, page 105.

11. Whitefield, *Journals*, page 67.

12. Letter from John Wesley to George Whitefield and his Friends at Oxford, 10 September 1736.

13. Whitefield, *Journals*, page 79.

14. Ibid., page 81.

15. Ibid., page 83.

16. Wesley, *Works*, quoted in Hindmarsh, *Evangelical Conversion Narrative*, page 121.

17. Letter from Howell Harris to George Whitefield, 8 January 1739, in Dallimore, *Whitefield*, vol. 1, page 234.

18. Dallimore, *Whitefield*, vol. 1, page 240.

19. Ibid., page 243.

20. Whitefield, *Journals*, page 216.

21. Ibid., page 216.

22. Ibid., page 228, Wednesday 7 March 1739.

23. Ibid., page 229.

24. Curnock, *Journal*, volume 2, page 167.

25. Ibid., pages 172–73.

26. Whitefield, *Journals*, page 243, Monday 2 April 1739.

27. Ibid., page 223, Sunday 25 February 1739.

28. Ibid., page 253, Tuesday 17 April 1739.

29. Ibid., page 243, Monday 2 April, 1739.

30. Ibid., page 251, Thursday 12 April, 1739.

31. Ibid., page 261, Sunday 29 April, 1739.

32. Quoted in G. Best, *Charles Wesley*, page 113.

33. Curnock, *Journal*, volume 2, Monday 30 April and Tuesday 1 May, 1739, pages 186–87.

34. Curnock, *Journal*, volume 2, Wednesday 2 May 1739, page 188.

Chapter 4: Dispute and division

1. Curnock, *Journal,* vol. 2, page 320, 15 November 1739.

2. Ibid., page 370, 20 July 1740.

3. Ibid., page 371, 23 July 1740, Wesley's spelling.

4. Whitefield, *Journal*, volume 3, 30 April 1739, page 261.

5. See George Whitefield's *Journals*, page 565, quoting L. Tyerman, *The Life and Times of John Wesley*.

6. Ibid.

7. Dallimore, *Whitefield*, vol. 1, page 433.

8. Whitefield, Letter, quoted in Dallimore, *Whitefield*, vol. 1, page 451.

9. Dallimore, *Whitefield,* vol. 1, page 451.

10. Quoted in Waller, *Wesley,* page 64.

11. Whitefield, Letter, 24 December 1740, *Journals*, page 571.

12. Ibid., page 574.

13. Ibid., page 588.

14. Curnock, *Journal*, vol. 2, page 439, Saturday 28 March 1741.

15. Dallimore, *Whitefield,* vol. 2, page 156.

16. Noll, *Rise of Evangelicalism,* page 118.

Chapter 5: Spreading the flame: The early pioneers

1. H. Venn, "Funeral Sermon for the Revd William Grimshaw", quoted in F. Cook, *William Grimshaw of Haworth,* Edinburgh: The Banner of Truth Trust, 1997, page 109.

2. Ibid., page 9.

3. H. Venn, "A Sketch of the Life and Ministry of the late Rev Mr Wm Grimshaw", quoted in Cook, *Grimshaw,* page 28.

4. Cook, *Grimshaw*, page 310.

5. Quoted in Cook, *Grimshaw,* page 75.

6. Noll, *Rise of Evangelicalism,* page 115.

7. Cook, *Grimshaw,* page 140.

8. *Journal of Charles Wesley*, quoted in Cook, *Grimshaw,* page 115.

9. Cook, *Grimshaw,* page 119.

10. Ibid., page 122.

11. Curnock, *Journal*, volume 3, 1 May 1747, page 293.

12. Ibid., 25 August 1748, page 371.

13. Cook, *Grimshaw,* page 133.

14. Whitefield, *Works*, vol. 2, page 282.

15. Ibid., page 448.

16. Curnock, *Journal*, volume 4, 25 August 1748, page 114.

17. Ibid., 22 May 1757, page 212–15.

18. Ibid., 22 July 1759, pages 332–33.

19. Ibid., 12 July 1761, pages 468–69.

20. G. R. Balleine, *History of Evangelical Party,* page 68, referring to the Letters of John Newton.

21. Cook, *Grimshaw,* page 272.

22. Ibid., page 135.

23. J. C. Ryle, *Five Christian Leaders of the Eighteenth Century*, London: Charles J. Thynne, 1902, page 327.

24. Ibid., page 308.

25. Balleine, *History of Evangelical Party*, page 96.

26. Ryle, *Christian Leaders of the Eighteenth Century*, page 310; Tim Shenton, *A Cornish Revival,* Darlington: Evangelical Press, 2003, page 53.

27. Shenton, *Cornish Revival,* page 55.

28. Ryle, *Christian Leaders of the Eighteenth Century,* page 311; Shenton, *Cornish Revival,* page 62.

29. Quoted in Shenton, *Cornish Revival,* page 68.

30. Shenton, *Cornish Revival,* page 74.

31. Ryle, *Christian Leaders of the Eighteenth Century,* page 316.

32. Ibid., page 318.

Chapter 6: The Countess and her circle

1. F. Cook, *Selina, Countess of Huntingdon*, Edinburgh: Banner of Truth Trust, 2001, page 37.
2. Ibid., page 37.
3. Quoted in Cook, *Selina,* pages 39–40.
4. Quoted in A. Harding, *Selina, Countess of Huntingdon,* Peterborough: Epworth, 2007, page 32.
5. Ibid., page 35.
6. Cook, *Selina,* page 70.
7. See Cook, *Selina,* page 93.
8. Quoted in Cook, *Selina,* page 94.
9. Dallimore, *Whitefield,* vol. 2, page 266.
10. Quoted in Harding, *Selina,* page 43.
11. Dallimore, *Whitefield,* vol. 2, page 269.
12. Harding, *Selina,* page 44.
13. Dallimore, *Whitefield,* vol. 2, page 273.
14. Noll, *Rise of Evagelicalism*, page 149.
15. Harding, *Selina,* page 51.
16. Ibid., page 54.
17. Ibid., page 179.
18. Quoted in Cook, *Selina,* page 375.
19. Ibid., page 422.

Chapter 7: The consolidation of the Revival

1. Peter Forsaith (ed.), *Unexampled Labours,* Epworth, 2008, pages 42–43.
2. Ibid., page 11.
3. *Letters of Henry Venn*, Edinburgh; Banner of Truth Trust, 1993, page 26.
4. M. M. Hennell, *Henry Venn of Huddersfield*, Churchman, 068/2, 1954, page 2.

5. Letter to Thomas Atkinson, 10 August 1764, in Venn, *Letters*, page 108.

6. J. Aitken, *John Newton*, Wheaton, IL: Crossway, 2007, page 272.

7. Forsaith, *Unexampled Labours,* page 117.

8. Ibid., page 93.

9. Ibid., pages 56–57.

10. Ibid., page 113.

11. Ibid., page 14.

12. Ibid., page 134.

13. Ibid., page 206.

14. W. Romaine, Letter CLXXXVI, *Works*, page 608.

15. Memoir, in Romaine, *Works*.

16. Aitken, *Newton*, page 151.

17. Ibid., page 176.

18. Letter to Charles Wesley, 8 June, 1762, Forsaith, *Unexampled Labours*, page 147.

19. Ibid., page 147.

20. Ibid.

21. Forsaith, *Unexampled Labours*, pages 53–54.

22. Ibid., page 147.

23. Venn, *Letters,* page 33.

24. Ibid., pages 32–33.

25. H. Venn, *The Complete Duty of Man*, Preface.

26. Forsaith, *Unexampled Labours*, page 242.

27. Ibid., page 253.

28. Ibid., page 259.

29. Ibid., page 270.

30. W. Romaine, Letter ii, *Works*, page 534.

31. W. Romaine, Letter XXXV, *Works*, page 550.

32. W. Romaine, Letter CLXXXVII, *Works*, page 603.

33. W. Romaine, Letter CCXLVI, *Works*, page 713.

34. W. Romaine, Letter CCXLVIII, *Works*, pages 716–17.

35. Letter to Mrs Medhurst, 11 September 1767, in Venn, *Letters*.

36. H. Venn, Letter to Mrs Riland, 17 November 1770, in Venn, *Letters*, page 165.

37. Venn, *Letters,* page 359.

38. Letter to Miss Wheeler of Kippax, in Venn, *Letters,* pages 120–21.

39. Letter to James Kershaw Esq., in Venn, *Letters,* page 159.

40. Forsaith, *Unexampled Labours*, page 20.

41. Memoir, in Romaine, *Works*, page 32.

42. Ibid.

43. Hennell, *Venn*, page 6.

44. Aitken, *Newton*, page 350.

Chapter 8: The maturing of the Revival

1. A. Bennett, *Charles Simeon, Prince of Evangelicals*, Churchman 102/2, 1988.

2. W. Carus, *Charles Simeon* (1847), page 703.

3. M. Hennell and A. Pollard (eds), *Charles Simeon 1759–1836* (1959), page 126.

4. A. Bennett, *Charles Simeon, Prince of Evangelicals*, Churchman 102/2, 1988.

5. W. Wilberforce, *A Practical View* (1797), Chapter II, pages 26–27.

6. R. D. Turnbull, *Shaftesbury: The Great Reformer,* Oxford: Lion Hudson, 2010.

7. Wesley, *Letters*, 10 September 1784 and quoted in Waller, *Wesley*, page 122.

8. Curnock, *Journal*, volume 7, Wednesday 1 September 1784.

9. Certificate of Ordination, in Curnock, *Journal*, volume 7.

10. Noll, *Rise of Evangelicalism*, page 192.

11. M. Watts, *The Dissenters,* Oxford: Clarendon Press, 1978, page 449.

Conclusion

1. M. Noll, *Rise of Evangelicalism,* page 281.

Appendix

1. J. D. Walsh. "Origins", page 132.

2. Ibid.

3. D. W. Bebbington, *Evangelicalism in Modern Britain,* London: Unwin Hyman, 1989, page 1.

4. D. W. Bebbington, in Michael Haykin and Kenneth Stewart (eds), *The Emergence of Evangelicalism,* Nottingham: Apollos, 2008, page 419.

5. Ibid., page 419.

6. W. M. Jacob, *The Clerical Profession in the Long Eighteenth Century, 1680–1840,* Oxford: OUP, 2007, page 7.

7. J. C. D. Clark, *English Society, 1660–1832,* Cambridge: CUP, second edition, 2000, page 17.

8. Walsh, "Origins", page 142.

9. Noll, *Rise of Evangelicalism*, page 44.

10. W. R. Ward, *The Protestant Evangelical Awakening*, Cambridge: CUP, 1992, page 296.

11. Campbell, *Religion of the Heart,* page 79.

12. Ibid., page 87.

13. Ibid.

14. J. D. Walsh, "'Methodism' and the origins of English-speaking Evangelicalism", in M. A. Noll, D. W. Bebbington and G. A. Rawlyk, *Evangelicalism*, New York: OUP, 1994, page 19.

15. Ibid., page 20.

16. Noll, *Rise of Evangelicalism*, page 45.

17. Ward, *Protestant Evangelical Awakening,* page 103.

Index